Contents

Preface

To the general reader

Although the *Access to History* series has been designed with the needs of students studying the subject at higher examination levels very much in mind, it also has a great deal to offer the general reader. The main body of the text (i.e. ignoring the Study Guides at the ends of chapters) forms a readable and yet stimulating survey of a coherent topic as studied by historians. However, each author's aim has not merely been to provide a clear explanation of what happened in the past (to interest and inform): it has also been assumed that most readers wish to be stimulated into thinking further about the topic and to form opinions of their own about the significance of the events that are described and discussed (to be challenged). Thus, although no prior knowledge of the topic is expected on the reader's part, she or he is treated as an intelligent and thinking person throughout. The author tends to share ideas and possibilities with the reader, rather than passing on numbers of so-called 'historical truths'.

To the student reader

There are many ways in which the series can be used by students studying History at a higher level. It will, therefore, be worthwhile thinking about your own study strategy before you start your work on this book. Obviously, your strategy will vary depending on the aim you have in mind, and the time for study that is available to you.

If, for example, you want to acquire a general overview of the topic in the shortest possible time, the following approach will probably be the most effective:

1 Read Chapter 1 and think about its contents.
2 Read the 'Making notes' section at the end of Chapter 2 and decide whether it is necessary for you to read this chapter.
3 If it is, read the chapter, stopping at each heading to note down the main points that have been made.
4 Repeat stage 2 (and stage 3 where appropriate) for all the other chapters.

If, however, your aim is to gain a thorough grasp of the topic, taking however much time is necessary to do so, you may benefit from carrying out the same procedure with each chapter, as follows:

1 Read the chapter as fast as you can, and preferably at one sitting.
2 Study the flow diagram at the end of the chapter, ensuring that you understand the general 'shape' of what you have just read.

3 Read the 'Making notes' section (and the 'Answering essay questions' section, if there is one) and decide what further work you need to do on the chapter. In particularly important sections of the book, this will involve reading the chapter a second time and stopping at each heading to think about (and to write a summary of) what you have just read.
4 Attempt the 'Source-based questions' section. It will sometimes be sufficient to think through your answers, but additional understanding will often be gained by forcing yourself to write them down.

When you have finished the main chapters of the book, study the 'Further Reading' section and decide what additional reading (if any) you will do on the topic.

This book has been designed to help make your studies both enjoyable and successful. If you can think of ways in which this could have been done more effectively, please write to tell me. In the meantime, I hope that you will gain greatly from your study of History.

Keith Randell

Acknowledgements

The Publishers would like to thank the following for permission to reproduce illustrations in this volume:

Cover - J.F. Kennedy with Khruschev in Vienna in 1961 (reproduced courtesy of Associated Press/Topham). Simon and Schuster, p. 80.

The publishers would like to thank the following for permission to reproduce copyright material:

André Deutsch for an extract from *Khruschev Remembers* S. Talbot (ed) (1971); Faber and Faber Ltd for extracts from *Mayday: Eisenhower, Khrushchev and the U-2 Affair* by M.R. Beschloss (1986); William Heinemann for extracts from *Waging Peace* by D.D. Eisenhower (1965); and W.W. Norton and Co Ltd for an extract from *Thirteen Days* by R. Kennedy.

Every effort has been made to trace and acknowledge ownership of copyright. The Publishers will be glad to make suitable arrangements with any copyright holders whom it has not been possible to contact.

CHAPTER 1

Overview: America and the Cold War, 1945-63

1 The United States and the Cold War, 1945-63: Introduction

On the morning of 1 May 1960 a supersonic plane stood on the runway of an American military base at Peshawar in Pakistan. The plane was a U-2 reconnaissance aircraft, a sophisticated piece of military hardware and an emblem of American high-technology. It had a range of 2,200 miles and could fly at an altitude of 13 miles beyond the range of enemy anti-aircraft missiles. It was fitted with a high-definition camera capable of capturing a readable image of a newspaper headline at a distance of ten miles. Since 1956 U-2s had been flying over the Soviet Union in secret, gathering valuable intelligence about Soviet military installations. For five years the Russians had been trying in vain to shoot one down. The pilot at the controls of U-2 Number 360 on that morning was Francis Gary Powers. He was about to embark on a flight over the Urals mountain range in the central Soviet Union which would end in Norway. Among other items packed into his flight suit was a silver dollar containing a shellfish toxin which caused instant death. U-2 pilots were under instructions to kill themselves if captured.

Within minutes of take-off Powers's plane soared to 60,000 feet and set off on its northward course. Powers entered Soviet airspace after an hour and flew over the Tyuratam Cosmodrome from where the Russians had launched several satellites into space. His next target was Sverdlovsk, a large industrial city. Suddenly Powers heard a thud and an orange flash engulfed his cockpit. His plane had been hit by a ground-to-air missile and went out of control. In a state of panic Powers struggled unsuccessfully to activate his ejector seat. He then realised he could escape his cockpit by opening the canopy above his head. He undid the canopy and was propelled into space. His orange and white parachute burst open and he fell to earth overtaken by fragments of his plane. When the dazed Powers hit the ground, he encountered a surprised Soviet farmer. The authorities were soon informed. In Moscow the Soviet leader Nikita Khrushchev was watching a parade in celebration of May Day, a traditional workers' holiday. He was told quietly about the triumph of the downed U-2. Meanwhile his American counterpart, President Eisenhower, did not find out about the disaster until the next day. A major Cold War crisis, the U-2 affair, was about to unfold.

The U-2 incident was an episode in the international conflict known as the Cold War. The term 'Cold War' had first been used about

Anglo-German rivalry between 1898 and 1914 and then about the frosty relationship between France and Germany in the 1930s. Broadly it means a state of permanent hostility between two powers which never erupts into an armed confrontation or a 'hot war'. In current historiography the term 'Cold War' describes the conflict between the Soviet Union and the United States from 1945 until 1989. It was popularised by the American journalist Walter Lippman in 1947 and widely used thereafter to describe US-Soviet relations.

The Cold War functioned at various levels. It was a confrontation between two vast continental states searching for power, influence and security. The form of the conflict had been anticipated by Adolf Hitler in his 'Testament' written in April 1945:

1 With the defeat of the Reich ... there will remain in the world only two Great Powers capable of confronting each other - the United States and Soviet Russia. The laws of both history and geography will compel these two powers to a trial of strength, either military 5 or in the fields of economics and ideology.

As Hitler had predicted, the Cold War was at one level a contest of ideas. By the late 1940s Soviet communism was seen as a demon by most Americans. They believed that America was waging the Cold War in order to protect and promote vital freedoms at home and abroad: freedom of expression, freedom of religion, freedom of conscience, free elections and free enterprise. Communist countries denied their people those fundamental freedoms and were 'police states'. The United States and its allies, on the other hand, represented the 'free world'. Americans were convinced of the inherent superiority of their system over the communist system. During a trip to the Soviet Union in 1959, Vice-President Richard Nixon visited a trade fair with the Soviet leader Nikita Khrushchev. A model American home was one of the exhibits. While walking around the display home, the two men engaged in an ongoing debate about the merits of communism and capitalism. The combative Khrushchev said, 'You are a lawyer for capitalism, I am a lawyer for communism. Let's compete.' Nixon portrayed America as a place of choice and freedom.

To us diversity, the right to choose ... is the most important thing. We don't have one decision made at the top by one government official. This is the difference.

Nixon then said the kitchen with its washing-machine and other labour-saving devices was typical of an American steelworker's home. His point was clear. America was not only a place of freedom and choice but a land of plenty. Capitalist America, not the communist Soviet Union, was able to deliver high living standards to the masses and had come closest to the Marxist ideal of an equal distribution of wealth. Khrushchev remained unconvinced. He had earlier boasted, 'in another seven years we will be on the same level as America. When we catch you up, in passing you by, we will wave to you.' The whole 'kitchen debate' nicely captured the battle of ideas underlying the Cold War.

For the United States the Cold War was also a quest for security and power. As early as 1946 the Americans treated the communist Soviet Union as an enemy. From the American perspective the Soviet Union had an inherent tendency to expand, since Marxism-Leninism (the Soviet version of Marxism) taught that capitalist and communist states could not co-exist. The Soviet Union would use its military resources and its control over national communist movements in Europe and Asia to extend its influence as far as possible. In American eyes all communist organisations were controlled from Moscow. International communism was always Soviet communism in another guise. US national security therefore depended on the containment of communism across the world. Alarmed by the occupation of eastern Europe and the Balkans by Soviet armies, the United States attempted to circumscribe Soviet power across the world as early as 1945. America was playing the role of a superpower, a great power with worldwide interests. In western Europe, the eastern Mediterranean, northern Iran and north-east Asia, the Americans wanted to stop the Soviet Union filling power vacuums created by the Second World War and prevent communist movements coming to power in the midst of political and economic chaos. The policy of confining communism to those areas where it already existed was called 'containment'. In the end very few areas of the world were untouched by the Cold War. The Middle East and the Americas south of the United States (Central America, South America and the Caribbean) later emerged as important arenas. In these areas the United States attempted to stop communist regimes coming to power or to remove existing communist governments. Indeed the greatest crisis of the Cold War, the Cuban Missile Crisis, had its origins in a successful communist coup in the Caribbean island of Cuba in 1959.

The United States saw the Cold War as a world power struggle with the Soviet Union. In the aftermath of the Second World War they were the two most powerful states and they formed the two poles of the international state system. Both nations were competing for a position of dominance within the system. The one and only enemy was the Soviet Union. Hence US officials viewed the Cold War as a bipolar conflict. The creation of the communist People's Republic of China in 1949 did not change their perception of the Cold War as bipolar. China was seen as a satellite of the Soviet Union and the threat posed by the two communist states was conflated and described as the 'Sino-Soviet threat'. It was only after the Sino-Soviet split in 1961 that the United States had to come to terms with the reality of two separate centres of communist power operating independently.

How did the Americans wage the Cold War? They employed every measure possible short of direct armed engagement with the Soviet Union. In the early stages of the conflict US dollars were the primary instrument of war. The United States exploited its status as the world's pre-eminent financial power to channel huge amounts of economic aid to its allies. The aims of economic assistance were to bolster non-communist governments threatened by communism and to subsidise the economic reconstruction of strategically important areas like west Germany and Japan. The economic resources of the United States in this period were truly vast. For example, between 1948 and 1952 the US granted $12.5 billion in economic aid to the states of western Europe.

The Americans also used military force to counter international communism, but not directly against the Soviet Union. When communist North Korean soldiers invaded South Korea in 1950 US forces were deployed immediately to drive back the North Koreans. The Korean War was the precursor of the Vietnam War. Twice during the Cold War the United States fought land wars in Asia in order to defeat international communism. After 1950 America was in a continuous state of military preparedness. Mobilisation for actual war may be regarded as one of the weapons of the Cold War and was intended to deter communist aggression. For the first time in their history the Americans maintained a large peacetime army, navy and air force. In 1960 there were 900,000 personnel in the US Army and 2.4 million men in the US armed forces as a whole. American servicemen were stationed across the globe in an attempt to confine communism. In 1959 the United States had 1,400 overseas military bases in 31 countries around the world. America's military commitments were worldwide in the era of the Cold War.

US armed forces were serviced by a massive nuclear arsenal. The Americans successfully developed an atom bomb in 1945 and by 1952 possessed a hydrogen bomb. The Soviet Union caught up quickly, testing an atom bomb in 1949 and a hydrogen bomb in 1953. Until 1963, however, the United States held an advantage over the Soviet Union in both the quantity and variety of its nuclear weapons. A fleet of B-47 and later B-52 bombers operated by the Strategic Air Command was available to deliver the bombs. As the Cold War progressed both the nuclear weapons and the delivery systems became more sophisticated. The evolution of ballistic (unmanned rockets) weapons brought the greatest change. By the end of the 1950s the United States owned short-range tactical nuclear missiles to be used on the battlefield, land-based intermediate-range ballistic missiles (IRBMs) with a range of between 1,500 and 3,000 nautical miles and intercontinental ballistic missiles (ICBMs) with a range in excess of 3,000 nautical miles. In 1960 the Americans also brought into service the Polaris submarine-based missile system. By 1963 there were more than 18,000 nuclear warheads in the US nuclear arsenal. The Soviet Union also possessed numerous nuclear weapons, but in the period covered by this book the United States always enjoyed an advantage in both the volume and the diversity of weapons in its nuclear arsenal. It was only in the early 1960s, for example, that the Soviet Union deployed its first ICBM.

In case of war the United States eagerly recruited friendly nations into alliance systems. Europe was effectively divided into American and Soviet spheres of influence by 1948, and in 1949 most of the nations of western Europe were organised into a military alliance called the North Atlantic Treaty Organisation (NATO), while the communist states of eastern Europe belonged to the Warsaw Pact after 1955. By the mid-1950s the Americans had built a global network of anti-communist military coalitions encompassing Latin America, western Europe, the Middle East, Australasia and southeast Asia.

Another traditional form of warfare employed by the Americans was economic warfare. After 1948 there was only a trickle of US exports to the Soviet Union and curbs were imposed on the sales of military equipment. America's allies in NATO introduced similar restrictions in 1953. The ongoing Cold War in trade was intended to keep Western military secrets from the Russians and to accelerate the downfall of the Soviet regime by denying the Soviet Union essential raw materials and manufactured goods.

Propaganda was also an important weapon in the Cold War. Two US-financed radio stations, Radio Liberty and Radio Free Europe, were set up in Germany to transmit Western news and values to countries in Soviet-controlled eastern Europe, the so-called eastern bloc. Dollars were also invested in West Berlin, a small Western enclave in the heart of communist East Germany, in order to turn the city into a showcase of Western affluence and a reminder to the people of East Germany of the prosperity they were missing.

Espionage, another old means of war, assumed a new importance during the Cold War. The Central Intelligence Agency (CIA) was set up in 1947 partly to co-ordinate information-gathering on the Soviet Union and its allies. In 1954 the CIA oversaw Operation Gold, the construction of a tunnel running from the US sector of Berlin into Soviet-controlled east Berlin. The tunnel allowed British and American engineers to tap coded telecommunications travelling to and from the Soviet Union's military and intelligence headquarters at Karlshorst. For two years the Americans eavesdropped on the Russians, collecting 1,200 hours of material daily, until the tunnel was stormed by Soviet troops in 1956. After 1956 the American U-2 spyplane provided invaluable intelligence about the Soviet Union, particularly the state of Soviet missile sites. A new form of surveillance was soon available in the form of satellites. The United States positioned its first satellite, *Discoverer,* in 1960 and launched *Samos I* the following year. Satellites revolutionised intelligence-gathering, since they were able to collect valuable information on the enemy without risking the lives of agents on the ground or U-2 pilots overflying the Soviet Union.

The CIA also conducted secret operations in order to combat communism. In the Italian elections of 1948 the objective of American policy was to prevent a communist victory at the polls. The election expenses of the principal non-communist party, the Christian Democrats, were paid by the US government via the CIA. The printing of anti-communist newspapers was subsidised by the Americans, and American grain was distributed to Italian peasants from trucks decorated in the colours of the Christian Democrats. Sometimes America's secret war against communism assumed more extreme forms. In the 1950s the CIA orchestrated the overthrow of left-wing governments in Iran and Guatemala and developed plans to murder the heads of communist foreign states. There is hard evidence of at least eight plots to assassinate the communist leader of Cuba, Fidel Castro. Castro was a prodigious smoker and one of the plots featured a box of poisoned cigars.

The Cold War is now over and forms a distinct era in post-war history. It was punctuated by crises and moments of high danger, but it was also a force for stability in world politics. The period of the Cold War has been called by some historians the 'long peace'. The following is an important historical fact: the United States and the Soviet Union never met on the battlefield. There were clear parameters to the conflict. Neither side tried or even wanted to invade the territory of the other. Similarly there was no attempt by either side to intervene by force in the other's sphere of influence. When East Germans rose against Soviet occupying forces in 1953 and Hungarians did the same in 1956, the United States took no action. Even in times of crisis both powers retreated from war. An important factor in the 'long peace' was undoubtedly the existence of nuclear weapons. A conventional war between the United States and the Soviet Union could quickly have become an unwinnable nuclear war. In the mid-1950s it was calculated that 65 per cent of the American population would require medical care following a nuclear exchange with the Soviet Union. President Eisenhower commented in 1955, 'It would literally be a business of digging ourselves out of the ashes, starting again.'

One of the benign consequences of the nuclear age was that it forced both America and the Soviet Union, unlike the great powers of the nineteenth century, to reject war as an instrument of policy against one another. It was simply too risky an option. The Cold War had to be waged by other means. This situation had been foreseen by the English author George Orwell. Reflecting on the implications of the atom bomb, he predicted an era 'as horribly stable as the slave empires of antiquity'. The great powers would not dare to go to war with each other, but would exist behind the shield of nuclear weapons 'unconquerable and in a permanent state of Cold War with neighbours'.

The Cold War also had a significant impact on the United States. It triggered important changes in the American political process. The powers of the president increased substantially. In particular Cold War presidents asserted ever more control over the making of foreign policy at the expense of Congress. The Cold War also left its mark on American society. The war against communism abroad became a war against communism at home. A wave of anti-communist paranoia swept the United States in the early 1950s. Proven communists were targeted, while at the same time people with no history of affiliation to communist groups were branded communists and interrogated by Congressional committees. Agents of the Soviet Union were seen everywhere. By the mid-1950s the 'Red Scare' had subsided and had been overtaken by a widespread anxiety about the effects of a nuclear exchange with the Soviet Union. A generation of Americans had to live with the fear of nuclear war. The economic effects of the Cold War were both good and bad. The rearmament of America after 1950 created a boom for the defence industry which contributed to wider economic growth. On the other hand, high defence spending caused federal budget deficits. The wealth of the United States meant it could sustain the costs of the Cold War, but even America found the economic burden of superpower status increasingly demanding. There is a detailed discussion of the overall impact of the Cold War on the United States in Chapter 7.

2 US Foreign Policy Making during the Cold War

Much of this book is about US foreign policy between 1945 and 1963 and this brief section is intended to give an insight into the American foreign policy making process in this period.

The president was the pivotal figure in the foreign policy process. All important foreign policy decisions were made by him and a few of his chosen aides. The authors of the constitution (written in 1787) had endowed the president with substantial powers in the field of foreign policy making. He was commander-in-chief of the armed forces, appointed and received ambassadors, appointed other key personnel, such as the Secretary of State, and made treaties with other states (although these had to be ratified subsequently by a two-thirds majority of the Senate). The president's position as head of state also tended to elevate him above party politics during foreign policy crises. At such times he was regarded as the figurehead of the nation and could draw on the patriotism and goodwill of the people.

The president was not a lone decision-maker in foreign policy matters. He relied on a small group of advisers from inside and outside government chosen because they enjoyed his trust and confidence. The Secretary of State (head of the State Department, which was responsible for US external relations and was the equivalent of the Foreign Office in the United Kingdom) was an especially important figure. The relationship between a president and his Secretary of State was vital to the conduct of foreign policy. The Defense Secretary, the Director of Central Intelligence (head of the CIA) and the Chairman of the Joint Chiefs of Staff, who gave the views of the armed services, were also usually members of the inner circle. The opinions of the latter were especially important when the president was considering the use of military force. The State Department, the Central Intelligence Agency, the National Security Council and the Defense Department (the last three all established in 1947) formed the second circle of the foreign policy establishment. All were responsible for funnelling information and advice to the president, implementing the decisions taken by the inner circle and, in the case of the State Department, for the day-to-day transaction of American foreign policy.

Congress, the American legislature, was the third important player in the making of foreign policy. Congress consisted of two chambers. The

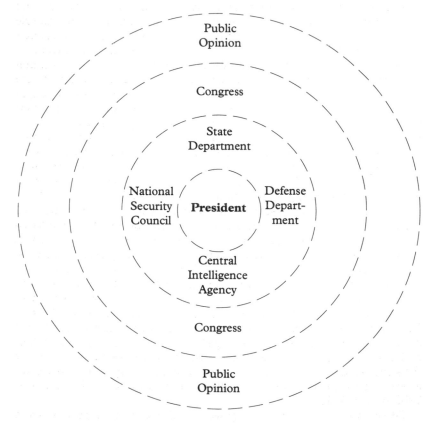

Influences on US foreign policy making, 1947-63

upper chamber was called the Senate. Each state elected two representatives to the Senate regardless of differences in population between states. The lower house was the House of Representatives. There each state was represented according to population. The powers of Congress over foreign policy had been clearly defined in the constitution. Only Congress had the right to declare war. In addition all foreign treaties concluded by the president were subject to approval by a two-thirds majority in the Senate. A network of committees existed in Congress whose function was to scrutinise the executive. One of the most important of these committees was the Senate Foreign Relations Committee, which had wide-ranging powers to call foreign policy-makers before it and question them on the conduct of policy. All the president's nominees to important foreign policy posts also had to be confirmed by the Senate.

The limits imposed on presidential powers by Congress had much to do with the historical background against which the constitution was produced. The constitution was intended as the basis for the government of a nation which had just liberated itself from British rule in a revolutionary war. It was essential that a president must not exercise the same wide-ranging executive powers as a British monarch. In particular he must not enjoy the sole authority to take the United States into war. Hence the power to declare war was exclusively vested in the legislature. The Founding Fathers also feared that a president might independently make alliances with foreign powers which might entangle the new nation in wars which were not in its interest. Thus the Senate must exercise an effective right of veto over any foreign treaties. Classically this was how the constitution was supposed to work, but the Cold War changed the balance of power between executive and legislature. After 1945 presidents wrested more and more control over war- and treaty-making from Congress (see Chapter 7).

Another potential constraint on the powers of a president was the belief of the constitution-makers in the clear separation of the functions of government. The legislature and the executive were created as separate entities. The president was not a member of Congress and was elected separately from members of Congress. Such a system could produce a situation where the president might belong to one party, while the majority in Congress belonged to another. A Republican president might have to deal with a Democrat Congress and vice versa. Unlike a British prime minister, an American president did not necessarily have a majority at his command in the legislature, prepared to vote as a bloc and willing to endorse government legislation. Consequently, securing the support of the opposition in Congress for his foreign policy was often a test of a president's political skills as he tried to assemble a majority behind his policies.

Often, however, foreign policy was not a matter of dispute between the two main parties, the Republicans and the Democrats, and a

Republican Congress willingly co-operated with a Democrat president and vice versa. There was a tacit understanding that party politics stopped at the water's edge. The result was that foreign policy was very often the product of co-operation between legislature and executive. This partnership between Congress and presidency was most apparent in the years 1946 to 1948 when a majority Republican Congress voted in favour of assistance to Greece and Turkey, dollar grants to western Europe and American membership of NATO, even though these were all the foreign policy initiatives of a Democrat president, Harry Truman. Between 1954 and 1960 there were also harmonious relations between a Democrat Congress and a Republican president, Dwight Eisenhower. The only exception was the period 1949-52 when a Republican Congress often fiercely criticised Truman's policies towards the Soviet Union and China.

The fourth and remotest influence on foreign policy was public opinion. This is not to suggest that public opinion was unimportant. One reason for Roosevelt's insistence on free elections in Poland throughout 1944 was his anxiety not to lose the support of Polish-Americans in the presidential election of that year. He believed that they would not vote for a candidate who had been seen to abandon Poland to the Soviet Union. Yet, in general, the American public responded positively to presidential leadership on foreign policy issues. In the period 1945 to 1963 there was broad public support for the anti-communist foreign policy pursued by successive administrations. Most Americans, for example, favoured intervention by US troops in Korea in 1950. Even when an American-backed invasion of communist Cuba in 1961 went disastrously wrong - the Bay of Pigs fiasco - the public rallied round President Kennedy. Instinctive popular anti-communism was undoubtedly a factor in public support for American foreign policy, but America's history of isolationism meant that many Americans were simply uninterested in or poorly informed about world events, and so were willing to be led by their president in such matters. In our period public opinion definitely had a limited impact on the formulation of foreign policy.

Making notes on '*Overview: America and the Cold War, 1945-63*'

The purpose of this chapter is to identify some broad themes and to provide a basic introduction to the US foreign policy making process. It might be a good idea to make brief notes on the first section in particular in order to enhance your understanding of the following chapters. If you do take notes, use the end-of-chapter diagram as a framework. After reading this chapter, you should be able to define the term 'Cold War', illustrate some of the key characteristics of the conflict and have some insight into the means used by the United States to wage the Cold War.

These are the areas your notes should concentrate on. You might also wish to take down the simplified diagram showing the key people and institutions in US foreign policy making.

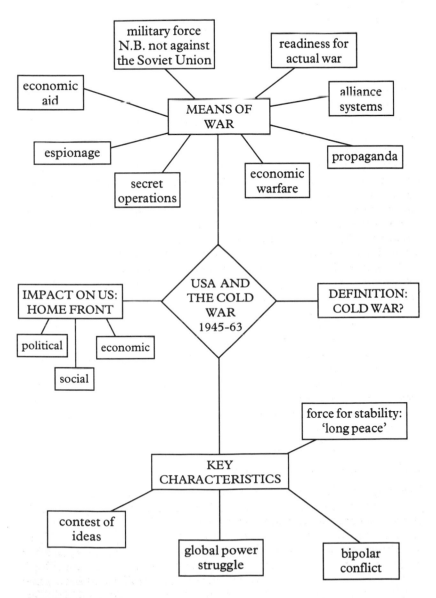

Summary - Overview: America and the Cold War, 1945-63

CHAPTER 2

Origins: The United States and the Beginning of the Cold War, 1945-6

1 Introduction

The Cold War is now over. But for nearly half a century the Cold War was the dominant feature of the world political landscape. An inquiry into how and why a historical process as complex and wide-ranging as the Cold War happened presents any historian with a formidable task. Ordinary wars begin when two nations engage in mutual organised violence, but the starting point of a conflict like the Cold War is less obvious. The argument of this chapter is that the conflict had discernible long-term causes, such as the historically uneasy relationship between America and Bolshevik Russia, and the very different ideas in both countries about the post-1945 world order. Moreover, US-Soviet friendship during the Second World War should perhaps be seen as above all an alliance of convenience whose strongest bond was a common interest in defeating Nazi Germany. Even during the war there were serious strains within the alliance and before the unconditional surrender of Germany in May 1945 those tensions were compounded by further disagreements on specific issues. The most serious division occurred on the question of Poland. Principally as a result of arguments about the political settlement of eastern Europe, US policy-makers in 1945 were already subject to two conflicting attitudes: a desire to continue the wartime partnership with the Russians and a profound suspicion of Soviet post-war ambitions both within Europe and beyond. The ambivalence of US policy in the immediate aftermath of war was soon replaced by new certainties. By 1946 the United States had abandoned a policy of long-term co-operation with the Russians and committed itself to the containment of Soviet power across the globe. The Soviet Union was seen as an enemy intent on territorial aggrandisement and ultimately world domination. It was in 1946 that the Cold War truly began.

2 Long-Term Causes of the Cold War

a) America and Russia 1917-41: Opposition and Recognition

The origins of the Cold War lie in the October Revolution of 1917, when Lenin and his Bolshevik Party seized power in Russia. As Lenin and the Bolsheviks rapidly laid the foundations of a one-party state, the US government watched events with alarm. The Americans had hoped that the revolution would be the beginning of an age of democracy in Russia. Fearful that Bolshevism would spread westwards into the defeated countries of post-First World War Europe, the United States and its allies made half-hearted and unsuccessful attempts to strangle the new Bolshevik regime in its infancy in 1919. American troops intervened briefly on the side of anti-Bolshevik forces in the Russian civil war.

The hostility of the United States to the world's first major communist state was grounded in American history and political culture. There was no tradition of left-wing politics in America. Neither of the main parties, the Republicans and Democrats, belonged to the left. Moreover, Marxism-Leninism as practised in Russia was very different from prevailing political ideals in the United States. A strong central state, one-party government, a command economy and a closed society were all at odds with the American belief in limited government, multi-party politics, individual rights, a free enterprise economy and an open society. Supporters of communism were regarded as extremists. When the American Communist Party was founded in 1919, it attracted attention out of all proportion to its size. Its activities were monitored by the federal government and its members were seen as agents of Bolshevik Russia intent on subverting American government from within. In 1919 a 'Red Scare' swept America and in January 1920 6,000 suspected communists were arrested and imprisoned. Many were later deported.

It was not until 1933 that there were formal diplomatic relations between the United States and Russia. Even then the rise of Japan in the Far East was an important factor in the decision of President Franklin Roosevelt to recognise the Soviet Union. An aggressive Japan threatened the national security of both America and the Soviet Union and both countries shared the objective of limiting Japanese power. After 1933 Soviet-American relations enjoyed a brief honeymoon but were soon strained by Stalin's methods of governing the Soviet Union. The 'show trials' of 1936, 1937 and 1938 had a particularly adverse impact on American public opinion. The use of fabricated evidence and confessions extracted under torture to sentence Stalin's political opponents to death was seen as typical of the way communist governments abused their power. Stalin's reputation suffered further damage when he concluded the Non-Aggression Pact with Hitler in August 1939 in order to save an unprepared Soviet Union from German invasion. Many Americans saw this as the work of two dictators with similar ideas and methods. They ignored the fact that the reluctance of the Western powers to conclude a defensive alliance with the Soviet Union against Nazi Germany had driven Stalin into the arms of Hitler.

The first quarter of a century of relations between the United States and the Soviet Union had been unpromising. The course of the Second World War, however, soon dictated that the two nations would be allies.

b) The United States and the Soviet Union 1941-4: Co-operation and Conflict

The German invasion of the Soviet Union in June 1941 immediately changed the relationship between America and the Soviet Union. Some Americans felt that Germany and Russia were as bad as one another and should be left to fight each other to a standstill. This view was not shared by President Roosevelt. America had not yet entered the war but was committed to the defeat of Nazi Germany. It must therefore help the Soviet Union as an enemy of Germany. Roosevelt also made a distinction between communist Russia and Nazi Germany. While the system of government in both countries was unpleasant to Americans, the important difference was that Russia had not acted aggressively like Hitler's Germany. All its actions had been defensive. In November 1941 America began to send supplies to the Soviet Union under the Lend-Lease Agreement. Under Lend-Lease America loaned the enemies of Germany military equipment for the duration of the war. The following month the Japanese bombing of Pearl Harbor brought America into the war as a belligerent. Japan's ally, Germany, also declared war on the United States. America was now an official ally of the Soviet Union in the war against Germany, but it was an alliance of convenience brought about by German and Japanese aggression. In the West the new partnership between the United States, Britain and the Soviet Union earned the grandiose title the 'Grand Alliance'. The Soviet term 'anti-Hitler coalition' was perhaps a more accurate description of the new relationship between the three states.

The wartime partnership between America and Russia was an effective one and achieved its ultimate objective of reducing Germany to unconditional surrender. American and Russian troops never fought alongside each other but America supplied the Soviet Union with ten million tons of Lend-Lease equipment. Soviet manpower and American money and military hardware defeated the German armies on the eastern front. Russia's long and bloody war with Germany also changed American attitudes towards the Soviet Union and its people. A fund of goodwill now existed towards Russia. In 1943 the American illustrated magazine *Life* sent a team of reporters to investigate conditions in the Soviet Union. Their report was favourable.

1 We have done this issue for one chief reason. We can help our
  readers to see and understand the Russian people. Like the US, the
  USSR is a huge melting pot, only in a different way. It contains 175
  nationalities speaking about 150 languages and dialects. What
5 brought all these people into one sovereign entity was the race of
  Great Russians, a talkative, aggressive and friendly mass of blond
  Slavs who have conquered and colonised a sixth of the earth's land

surfaces. They had crossed Siberia and reached the Pacific 300 years ago. They will go anywhere and try anything. They were one
10 hell of a people long before the revolution. To a remarkable degree, they look like Americans, dress like Americans and think like Americans. Today the USSR ranks among the top three or four nations in industrial power. She has improved her health, built
15 libraries, raised her literacy to about 80 per cent and trained one of the most formidable armies on earth. If the Soviet leaders tell us that the control of information was necessary to get this job done, we can afford to take their word for it for the time being.

Yet there were cracks in the Soviet-American alliance. The two sides argued about the opening of a second front against Germany. Stalin wanted the United States and Britain to invade western Europe in order to relieve pressure on the Red Army in the east. As early as 1942 Roosevelt promised a second front but the repeated postponement of plans for an Anglo-American invasion of German-occupied France angered Stalin. Britain and America meanwhile deployed their armies in North Africa and Italy and delayed an invasion of France across the Channel until D-Day in June 1944. Stalin also feared that America and Britain would conclude a separate peace with Nazi Germany and that the three of them would then turn their forces against communist Russia. Stalin's suspicion of his allies was sometimes reciprocated. In 1941 American scientists had begun work on the development of an atomic bomb in a programme called the Manhattan Project. Roosevelt decided to share some information about the project with Britain and Canada but not to tell the Soviet Union about it. This decision hardly showed a high level of trust in one of America's allies. Furthermore Stalin knew that Russia was being denied knowledge of the bomb because Soviet spies had infiltrated the team of American scientists developing the bomb.

The Second World War was a period of unprecedented co-operation between the United States and the Soviet Union. The Grand Alliance brought about the defeat of Nazi Germany. Nevertheless residual mutual suspicion and disagreement on specific issues such as the second front suggested that the two sides might find making the peace together harder than winning the war together. Before the war's end further serious divisions arose. They will be discussed in detail in section 2. To understand how the wartime alliance disintegrated so quickly we now need to examine the post-war aims of the Americans and the Russians.

c) Peace Aims

Roosevelt and Stalin shared some post-war objectives. Both agreed on the importance of limiting the power of Germany. German disarmament and demilitarisation would be achieved by military occupation.

The United States and the Soviet Union had agreed in principle to divide and occupy Germany among the victors. Both sides also shared the goal of continued co-operation after the war. Roosevelt even thought that Russia might be a more important ally to the United States than Britain; Stalin genuinely wanted to remain on good terms with America.

Roosevelt's Key Post-War Aims

- international peace and co-operation (UN)
- no formal spheres of influence
- spread of democracy (free speech, free elections)
- free trade (Open Door)
- reconstruction of world economy (IMF, World Bank)

Yet in many respects Russian and American plans for the post-war world were radically different. Roosevelt had a clear programme for peace. Perhaps his most cherished objective was the creation of a world peace-keeping organisation, the United Nations. He also wanted no empires or spheres of influence in the post-war world. A sphere of influence is a group of states under the indirect control of an outside power. Roosevelt believed that all states had a right to self-determination (to decide for themselves how they would be governed). Within post-war states he also hoped that democratic institutions would flourish and that people would enjoy the human rights of free speech and free elections. America's commitment to the principles of self-determination, free speech and free elections was based partly on national experience. The United States had rejected colonial rule by Britain and had been a free and independent state since 1776. There was a long tradition of individual liberty and freedom of expression within the United States, at least for white Americans. Their own history and experience inclined Americans to believe that democracy was a morally superior system of government. Furthermore, many Americans believed they had a mission to export democratic values to the rest of the world. Roosevelt's adviser, Harry Hopkins, clearly expressed these views in 1945.

1 I think we have the most important business in the world. And that is this - to do everything within our diplomatic power to foster and encourage democratic government throughout the world. We should not be timid about blazoning to the world our desire for the
5 right of all peoples to have a genuine civil liberty. We believe our dynamic democracy is the best in the world.

The United States also had fixed ideas about the shape of the world economy after the war. Free trade, the unrestricted exchange of goods between nations, was especially important. Individual countries should operate an 'Open Door' policy, opening their markets to imported goods. National economies should also be organised around the principles of the free market. Production and distribution of goods should be the responsibility of the private sector and not the state. At the Bretton Woods Conference in 1944 America had laid plans for the creation of two institutions, the International Monetary Fund (IMF) and the World Bank, which would shape an open world economy after the war. Both would act as lenders to defeated countries which were interested in adopting free trade policies and building market economies.

America's support for the Open Door was rooted in both idealism and self-interest. Americans genuinely believed that the free exchange of goods between nations maximised the volume of world trade and worldwide prosperity. Free trade also contributed to world peace. Nations which traded with each other were less likely to make war on each other. An international regime of free trade also created a vast world marketplace for American goods. Between 1940 and 1944 American industrial output had grown by 90 per cent and American policy-makers were worried that the end of the war would bring a collapse in world demand for American products and a return to the Depression of the 1930s.

Stalin's Key Post-War Aims

- co-operation with America
- Russian security
- sphere of influence on Soviet perimeter
- restoration of Russia's 1914 borders
- limiting German power
- economic reconstruction of Soviet Union

Stalin's overriding concern after the war was the security of the Soviet Union. Russia had paid a high price for victory over Germany. Fifteen million soldiers and 10 million civilians had died and 1,700 towns, 31,000 factories and 100,000 state farms had been destroyed. Twice in Stalin's lifetime Germany had invaded Russia from the west. His chief objective was therefore to guarantee the future safety of the Soviet Union firstly by moving its boundaries westward and restoring its 1914 borders, and secondly by creating a belt of friendly states on Russia's western perimeter. Poland, Romania and Bulgaria would form a Soviet sphere of influence and a security cordon against German expansion. Stalin's fear of Germany was never fully understood in the United

States. American insensitivity to Russian insecurity was partly the product of geography and history. America was a vast continental state protected on both sides by huge oceans. Its neighbours, Canada and Mexico, posed no military and economic threat and the United States had not been invaded and occupied since the War of 1812 with Britain.

From Stalin's point of view it was essential that the eastern European states forming Russia's security barrier should have similar political and economic systems to those of the Soviet Union. He believed that the Red Army's occupation of Poland, Romania and Bulgaria gave him the right to determine what sort of governments existed there. He made this plain in 1945.

> Whoever occupies a territory also imposes on it his own social system. Everyone imposes his own system as far as his army has power to do so. It cannot be otherwise.

The American programme for the post-war world of free speech, free elections and an 'Open Door' was therefore not acceptable in eastern Europe to Stalin on security grounds. It was also alien to Russia's traditions and history. Democracy and free speech had never existed in Russia either under the Tsars or under the Bolsheviks. Lenin had set up a one-party state based on the doctrine of the 'leading role of the party'. Free speech and dissent were not tolerated either within the Communist Party or in Russian society at large. The ideas of a free market and free trade were similarly unfamiliar to Russians. The Soviet economy was controlled by the State. In 1928 Stalin had launched a series of Five Year Plans in which production targets, investment, wage levels and the distribution of goods were all directed by central government. Nor had the Soviet Union practised the policy of the 'Open Door' before the war. On the contrary, Stalin had isolated the Russian economy from the rest of the world.

Stalin was also less concerned than Roosevelt about world peace and the reconstruction of the world economy. At the San Francisco Conference in May 1945 the Soviet Union did join the UN. Stalin was wary of international organisations and sceptical about the ability of bodies like the UN to keep peace, but he consented to Soviet participation because he was satisfied that membership would not endanger Soviet security. As a permanent member of the five-nation UN Security Council, Russia had the right to veto any UN decision contrary to its interests. The Soviet Union had also provisionally agreed to join the IMF and the World Bank at the Bretton Woods Conference in 1944, though Stalin was worried that both organisations might interfere with the internal management of the Soviet economy. Stalin hoped that he would be able to work outside these institutions and approach the United States directly for loans to finance Russian economic recovery. In this way the continuation of the US-Soviet alliance would bring real benefits to the Soviet Union.

Several important points emerge from a study of Soviet and American peace aims. Firstly, the differences between the post-war objectives of the two sides were more obvious than the similarities. Their contrasting visions of the world after the war reflected different value systems, different historical experiences and different security requirements. Secondly, America's peace plans were global in scope. The United States hoped to reshape the world into a community of democratic, independent and free-trading nations through new American-led institutions such as the UN, the World Bank and the IMF. This has been described as a 'one world' policy. The 'one world' vision of the Americans embraced the Soviet Union's neighbours in eastern Europe and it was in Poland where the US design for a new post-war world order first clashed with the Soviet Union's more limited objective of creating a sphere of influence on its borders.

3 The Breakdown of the US-Soviet Alliance, 1945: Key Issues

a) Poland

The situation in Poland was complex. After the partition of Poland between Germany and Russia in 1939 the Polish government fled to London. The absentee Polish government was known as the London Poles. Both the United States and Britain recognised the London Poles as the official government, but the Soviet Union ended relations with them in 1943 after they had criticised Stalin. Stalin later exploited the Red Army's occupation of Poland in 1944 to set up a pro-Soviet government called the Lublin Committee and to fix Russia's boundaries with Poland where they had been in 1914.

The Polish question was discussed by Stalin, Roosevelt and Churchill at the Big Three Yalta Conference in the Crimea in February 1945. Both Churchill and Roosevelt objected to the revision of Poland's eastern border and asked for the inclusion of the London Poles in the Lublin Committee, to be closely followed by free Polish elections. Stalin was furious with Anglo-American interference in the affairs of a country he regarded as vital to Russian security. He also could not understand why Britain and the United States were reopening an issue which he believed had been settled at previous wartime meetings. With good reason Stalin believed that his allies had already conceded a sphere of influence to him in eastern Europe.

At the Big Three Conference in Tehran in 1943 Churchill had suggested a permanent change in eastern Europe's frontiers. Russia could regain her 1914 boundaries by absorbing eastern Poland, while Poland would be compensated by receiving parts of eastern Germany.

In other words, the borders of Russia and Poland would be shifted westward at Germany's expense and to the advantage of the Soviet Union. Churchill had illustrated the revision of national boundaries in eastern Europe with matchsticks. When Roosevelt heard of this plan, he did not object but said that he could not publicly agree in case he alienated the Polish-Americans whose votes he needed at the 1944 presidential election. In October 1944 Stalin and Churchill held a bilateral meeting in Moscow at which an informal percentages agreement was concluded: Britain would have 90 per cent influence in Greece, in return Russia would enjoy 90 per cent influence in Romania and 75 per cent in Bulgaria. Roosevelt was not present in Moscow but an American observer attended the meeting. Roosevelt was certainly briefed on the outlines of the percentages deal and never openly opposed the informal agreement reached at the Moscow meeting. It is hardly surprising, therefore, that the Tehran and Moscow agreements formed the guidelines for Soviet policy in eastern Europe.

To some extent Roosevelt was responsible for the Polish dispute. The American president contributed to the misunderstanding over Poland in two ways. In order to secure continuing Soviet co-operation in the war effort he appeared to endorse a Soviet sphere of influence in eastern Europe in 1943 and 1944, only later to insist that the area should be

Poland in 1945

open to American influence and follow the American pattern of free elections and representative government. American demands at Yalta were an attempt to retrieve what had been given away at previous meetings with Stalin. US policy was therefore inconsistent. Secondly, Roosevelt kept the private wartime deals with Stalin on eastern Europe secret from the American people, while in public the president and his Secretary of State, Cordell Hull, continued to trumpet their vision of a post-war world without spheres of influence. On his return from Yalta, Roosevelt, by now a very sick man, addressed both Houses of Congress and announced that the Americans had got their way over Poland. It was an optimistic and highly misleading version of the Yalta negotiations. Consequently, there was a gulf between American expectations of Soviet policy in eastern Europe and actual Soviet policy. When Stalin failed to carry out the Yalta accords to the letter, suspicion about Soviet motives intensified within the United States. The ambiguities of Roosevelt's diplomacy not only confused Stalin but misled the American public.

Stalin did promise at Yalta to broaden the Lublin Committee through the inclusion of some London Poles and to hold free elections. Yet such undertakings raised problems of interpretation, since the Soviet Union and the United States read different meanings into the terms 'democracy' and 'free elections'. Stalin also signed the Declaration of Liberated Europe which pledged free elections and democratic institutions to countries freed from Nazi occupation, but he saw the Declaration as a statement of intent and not a legally binding document. He attached much more importance to agreements of the sort concluded with Churchill in Moscow, which took account of the realities of power. The eastern Mediterranean had historically been an area of British influence, while Romania and Bulgaria had traditionally formed a defensive curtain on Russia's south-western frontier. Hence he was prepared to trade British control in Greece for Soviet domination over Romania and Bulgaria. He once confided to the other two wartime leaders that he understood accords like the percentages deal as practical arithmetic, whereas vague statements such as the Declaration of Liberated Europe were merely algebra to him.

After Yalta the Russians did not conduct free elections in Poland. The Polish question was eventually settled in June 1945 when, in return for the addition of some London Poles to the mainly communist Polish Government of National Unity, the United States recognised the new Poland. The Soviet Union's new western border with Poland remained in place. Stalin's minor concessions fell short of American demands, but the United States was powerless to influence events in Poland. The Red Army's occupation of Poland was a fact and Stalin could do what he liked there. Soviet-American differences over Poland were an important cause of the Cold War. They led Roosevelt shortly before his death in April 1945 to doubt for the first time the possibility of post-war co-operation with the Russians. As a result of the failure to hold free elections in Poland, Roosevelt's successor, Harry Truman, lectured the Soviet Foreign Minister, Molotov, on the importance of honouring agreements. Molotov complained that he had never been treated so roughly at an official meeting. 'Carry out your agreements and you won't get talked to like that', retorted Truman. The dispute over Poland had created an atmosphere of mistrust and suspicion between the two sides. It also carried a wider significance. American policy-makers saw the Polish question as an acid test of Soviet intentions. The failure to hold elections was a breach of good faith and caused fear in Washington. Policy-makers worried that the Soviet Union was intent on projecting its power into new areas. Officials therefore concluded that while it was impossible to thwart Soviet ambitions in eastern Europe, the United States must contain Soviet power elsewhere. The consequences of such a policy were soon in evidence.

b) Economic Reconstruction

The Soviet Union had provisionally agreed to join the World Bank and the IMF at the Bretton Woods Conference in 1944. Stalin had reservations but the promise of a post-war loan from the United States persuaded him to go along with US plans for the world economy after the war. However, the provision of American capital to finance the rebuilding of the Soviet Union soon became a contentious issue. In January 1945 the Russians asked for a $6 billion loan. The Americans immediately imposed conditions on such a loan, in particular the opening of eastern European markets to US manufactured products. The United States was using its financial muscle to extract political concessions, a strategy known as dollar diplomacy. The Russians did not yield to such pressure tactics, and Molotov told the Americans that Russian soldiers had not sacrificed their lives during the war so that eastern Europe could be flooded with American films and magazines and US dollars.

The termination of Lend-Lease without notice in May 1945 was also a source of tension. It was not intended as a snub to the Russians but as an economy measure. Lend-Lease was a misleading name. In fact, the United States had been gifting dollars and equipment to the Russians and Truman calculated that the American taxpayer would no longer be prepared to finance aid to the Soviet Union in peacetime. For their part, the Russians had hoped that the flow of capital and equipment would continue at least in the short term and would lay the foundations for economic recovery in the Soviet Union. In order to promote economic reconstruction the Soviet Union made a further request for a loan in August 1945 which was mysteriously lost by the State Department. It appeared to the Russians that the United States was unwilling to collaborate in post-war economic reconstruction, and the December

1945 deadline for membership of the IMF and World Bank passed without the Russians joining.

A combination of the tough conditions attached to post-war US loans, the abrupt termination of Lend-Lease and the dispute over Poland resulted in the Soviet Union boycotting both organisations. The Soviet Union was not prepared to be part of the open world economy desired by the Americans. Its refusal to participate in a global economic system increased the likelihood of a separate economic bloc in eastern Europe under Soviet leadership.

c) Atomic Weapons

Truman's first encounter with Stalin was at the Potsdam Conference in July 1945. The central purpose of the conference was to discuss the occupation of Germany but the proceedings were overshadowed by a momentous event. On 16 July an atomic bomb was successfully exploded by the Americans in the New Mexico desert and the atomic age began. American scientists had been developing the bomb since 1941 in a programme known as the Manhattan Project. Eight days after the successful testing of the bomb, Truman casually informed Stalin that the United States now possessed a new weapon of enormous destructive power. Stalin pretended to be unconcerned and wished the Americans luck with its use against Japan, but he was also deeply worried by America's sole possession of the bomb - the atomic monopoly. The availability of such a weapon to the United States alone presaged a permanent shift in the balance of world power, and Stalin quickly authorised an accelerated atomic weapons programme in the Soviet Union.

The availability of the atom bomb immediately influenced American attitudes towards Soviet participation in the Pacific war against Japan. The defeat of Japan was proving more difficult than the defeat of Germany and in 1945 the US military thought that victory against Japan might take another year. At Yalta Roosevelt therefore secured a promise from Stalin that the Soviet Union would enter the war against Japan within three months of the surrender of Germany. By July, however, both Truman and his Secretary of State, James Byrnes, hoped that the bomb would enable the United States to defeat Japan without Russia. Differences over Poland had convinced some policy-makers that the Soviet Union wanted to exploit its position as victor to expand its borders. Soviet participation in the war against Japan would be followed by demands for a role in the post-war occupation of Japan and territorial claims in north-east Asia. While there is little supporting evidence that the Americans dropped the atomic bombs on Hiroshima and Nagasaki to frighten the Russians, they certainly saw the bomb as a useful means of ending the war with Japan before the Russians intervened.

The United States attempted to turn the atom bomb not only to military but to diplomatic advantage, using it as a bargaining counter in negotiations. Truman believed that America's atomic monopoly would enable him to achieve much of what he wanted at the negotiating table. Observers reported a new vigour and confidence in him once news of the test had reached Potsdam. He himself reported that he was 'tremendously pepped up' by news of the test. His Secretary of State, James Byrnes, thought that the bomb 'had given us great power and in the last analysis it would control'. The Americans now offered information about the bomb in return for the reorganisation of Soviet-controlled governments in Romania and Bulgaria. The tactic of trading the secret of the bomb for political concessions has been called atomic diplomacy. But the bomb proved to be a blunt instrument of diplomacy as the Russians refused to be intimidated into concessions. At the meeting of foreign ministers in London in September 1945, Molotov ridiculed the Americans' new weapon, but his mockery concealed both fear and resentment of American negotiating tactics.

d) Germany

At the Yalta Conference the Big Three had decided to divide post-war Germany into four zones of occupation. The fourth zone was allocated to France. Two more important decisions about Germany were taken at the Potsdam Conference. Firstly, it was agreed that each occupying power would be entitled to take reparations from its own zone. These reparations were intended as compensation for human, material and financial losses incurred in the war against Germany and were to take the form of industrial output and equipment. The extent of Soviet war losses was recognised in an agreement whereby the Russians were granted additional reparations from the three western zones in exchange for food and raw materials from the Soviet zone. The precise amount of reparations the Russians would receive had not been fixed, but a figure of $10 billion had been agreed at Yalta as the starting-point for negotiations. Secondly, the occupying powers agreed to treat the four zones of occupation as a single economic area. In other words goods were supposed to move freely between the four zones. The occupation of Germany was therefore a real test of the ability of the United States and the Soviet Union to co-operate in the day-to-day administration of a defeated country.

However, the two sides quickly encountered difficulties in carrying out a joint occupation policy. German coal ouput was an important area of disagreement. The Russians wanted coal from the western zones as reparations, but the Americans wanted to use German coal to assist in the economic reconstruction of western Europe. Policy-makers believed that Europe in 1945 was on the brink of collapse. US visitors to the continent were shocked by the extent of physical damage, the number of refugees, low civilian morale and the breakdown of ordinary economic activity. Pessimistic Americans foresaw the end of European civilisation and the onset of anarchy. In such circumstances, communism might sweep the continent. Consequently, German coal reserves must be quickly mobilised to service European economic recovery. Truman instructed General Eisenhower, commander of US forces in Europe, to make the mining and export of 25 millions tons of west German coal by April 1946 the paramount objective of occupation policy. Soviet reparations claims had to take second place to the energy requirements of the war-torn states of central and western Europe.

Soviet occupation policy also caused friction. The Russians were treating their zone as a self-contained economic entity which existed exclusively for their economic benefit. German factories were dismantled and moved piecemeal to the Soviet Union. Punishment and economic exploitation were the guiding principles of Soviet occupation policy. Some reparations from the British and American zones had been delivered to the Russians, but the Soviet Union was not supplying food and basic commodities in return. The Americans insisted that they would not send more reparations until the Russians exported essential items from their zone. Food, clothing, timber and machinery from eastern Germany were needed in the west to sustain the Ruhr workforce

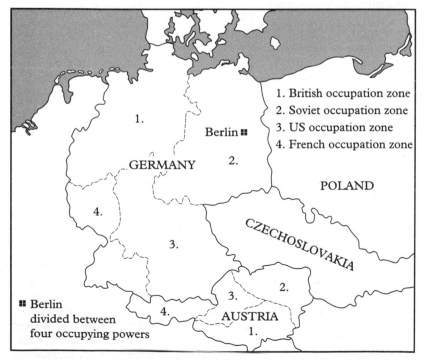

1. British occupation zone
2. Soviet occupation zone
3. US occupation zone
4. French occupation zone

Berlin ::

GERMANY

POLAND

CZECHOSLOVAKIA

:: Berlin
divided between
four occupying powers

AUSTRIA

Occupied Germany 1945

and re-equip the mines. In turn, the Russians argued that they would not release goods from their zone until they received a satisfactory level of reparations. Just as each side had interpreted the Yalta accords on Poland differently, so they read different meanings into the Potsdam agreements on Germany. The difficulty in implementing and interpreting agreements was a significant cause of the Cold War.

Access to the coal and steel output of the Ruhr valley, west Germany's industrial heartland, was a further cause of conflict. The Russians demanded four-power international control over the Ruhr, which lay inside the British zone of occupation. Both the British and the Americans refused Soviet demands for international trusteeship of the Ruhr. On account of Soviet actions in eastern Europe and the Soviet refusal to allow exports from their zone, they were wary of granting the Soviets any rights outside their own zone of occupation. It was too dangerous to give the Soviet Union a foothold in the western half of Germany. A State Department paper warned that 'under present circumstances an extension of Soviet power into the heart of Western Europe through the device of trusteeship would manifestly be open to grave doubt'.

4 1945: The United States and the Search for Security

The on-going failure of the United States and the Soviet Union to settle the major issues of the post-war world deepened American suspicion about Soviet motives. The Soviet occupation of eastern Europe in particular was seen as a prelude to Soviet expansion elsewhere. The United States now took a number of measures to enhance its national security in the face of a perceived potential Soviet threat. The Americans did not want to harm the Soviet Union and wanted to continue the wartime partnership, but at the same time they sought to prevent the extension of Soviet military power into areas deemed vital to US interests.

One of the first attempts to block Soviet expansion occurred in Manchuria. The backcloth to events there was a civil war between the Chinese Nationalists or Kuomintang (KMT) under Jiang Jieshi (Chiang Kai-shek) and the Chinese Communist Party (CCP) led by Mao Zedong (Mao Tse-tung). The Chinese civil war had begun in the 1920s. In the 1930s both sides had placed country before party and formed a united front to drive the Japanese out of China. Following Japan's defeat in 1945 they resumed their battle for the control of China.

Only a few days before the Japanese surrender the Soviet Union entered the war against Japan and moved troops into neighbouring Manchuria ostensibly to disarm Japanese soldiers. Stalin recognised Jiang's Nationalists as the legitimate government of China and quickly acknowledged Chinese sovereignty over Manchuria, but in the short term he moved to safeguard Soviet interests there. Soviet commanders handed weapons given up by Japanese soldiers over to CCP units and allowed the Chinese communists to establish a foothold in Manchuria and northern China. Manchuria was adjacent to the Soviet Union and CCP control of the region was preferable to its domination by the American-backed KMT. Although links between the Kremlin and the CCP had always been tenuous, the CCP might also prove useful allies in the event of the breakdown of the US–Soviet alliance and attempts by the United States to exert excessive influence over Chinese affairs through their ally, Jiang Jieshi.

Soviet actions in Manchuria brought a swift response from the United States. In September 1945 50,000 US Marines were sent to northern China to secure key communications centres and road and rail routes and to help transport Nationalist armies to the area. The Americans wanted the KMT to establish a strong presence in northern China. Old anxieties about Japanese power in the Far East were now superseded by a new fear of Soviet power. American officials worried that the Russians and their erstwhile allies the CCP would fill the vacuum left in Manchuria by Japan. Soviet behaviour in eastern Europe had convinced policy-makers that Russia wanted to extend its influence well beyond the Sino-Soviet border into north-east Asia. Washington was firmly committed to the containment of CCP/Soviet influence in the region.

The United States retained a close interest in northern China. In December 1945 George Marshall was appointed as ambassador to China. His brief was clear: to arrange a truce between the CCP and the KMT in the renewed civil war, to ensure Nationalist domination of Manchuria, to secure the withdrawal of Soviet troops from there and to oversee the creation of a coalition government with authority over all of China. Within this government the Nationalists would form the majority. The Americans wanted the KMT to be the dominant force in Chinese politics and to marginalise the CCP. Marshall was in any case suspicious of the CCP and saw Mao's party as an arm of Soviet communism. At the end of 1945 America's overall goal was a unified and stable China well disposed towards the United States in which the CCP had as little influence as possible.

Washington worried about Soviet intentions elsewhere in north-east Asia. In August 1945 Soviet troops had moved across the Russian border into northern Korea. The Americans were keen to prevent Soviet control over the entire Korean peninsula and quickly despatched troops to southern Korea. Stalin did not object and the two sides agreed to divide Korea into two occupation zones along the 38th parallel. The Russians occupied the industrial north, the Americans the agricultural south. The communist Kim Il Sung headed the administration in the north, while in the south an anti-Soviet nationalist Syngman Rhee established himself in power with American backing.

As early as 1945 the United States also tried to baulk Soviet advances in the Middle East and the eastern Mediterranean. Under wartime agreements Russian troops had been garrisoned in Iran in order to stop a seizure of the Persian oilfields by the Axis powers. After the war Soviet troops remained in Iran and encouraged separatist movements in the northern provinces of Azerbaijan and Kurdistan. It appeared to the United States that Stalin was attempting to create a sphere of influence on the Soviet Union's southern perimeter similar to the one emerging on Russia's western borders. The Americans and the British were determined to exclude the Soviet Union from Iran and preserve the country as a vital buffer between Russia and the oilfields of the Middle East. At the meeting of foreign ministers in Moscow in December 1945 Britain and America protested at the continued presence of Russian troops in Iran and reminded the Russians that the agreed date for withdrawal was 1 March 1946.

Washington was also concerned about the creeping advance of communism in the Mediterranean. In Yugoslavia communists under Josip Broz Tito had played a key role in defeating the Germans and had emerged as the dominant force in the country by 1945. In May 1945 Tito's forces reached Trieste, a port city whose ownership had historically been disputed between Italy and Yugoslavia. The Americans wanted to prevent an important outlet into the Adriatic Sea falling into the hands of communists and to retain Trieste within Italian borders. They protested to both Stalin and Tito about the movement of Yugoslavian forces into Trieste and Tito withdrew his troops. Trieste became an independent free city until 1955. In Greece the withdrawal of German armies had been followed by a civil war between the right and the left. The Americans feared a takeover by the Greek Communists (KKE), particularly in view of the presence of Soviet occupation armies in the rest of the Balkans and Tito's control of Yugoslavia. Accordingly, the United States made a $25 million loan to Greece in an attempt to stabilise the economy and prevent a political revolution which they believed the KKE might exploit.

5 1946: New Perceptions of the Soviet Union

In 1945 the attitudes of US officials towards the Soviet Union had become increasingly equivocal. A predisposition to collaborate with the Russians in making the peace had co-existed with a desire to curb Soviet power in certain areas of the world. Consequently American policy was inconsistent. Indeed throughout 1945 Washington was searching for a coherent policy towards the Kremlin. During 1946 American perceptions of the Soviet Union changed for the worse. New views of the Soviet Union prompted a turn in US policy. From the opening months of 1946 the Soviet Union was seen no longer as an ally but as a potential adversary.

George Kennan, an official in the US Embassy in Moscow, was instrumental in changing attitudes towards the Russians. On 22

February 1946 he sent the State Department a telegram which offered a historical analysis of the motives of Soviet foreign policy. Kennan argued that Russian rulers had always been weak and exerted limited authority over their people. Therefore they needed to invent an external enemy in order to unite the Russian people behind them. The enemy was the West. Historically Russian rulers had feared contact with and invasion from that quarter. Their response was to fix Russian borders as far west as possible. Kennan's analysis went a stage further. Marxism-Leninism had taken root in the Soviet Union precisely because it taught that communist states could not co-exist peacefully with capitalist states. It therefore justified the continuation of the historic state of conflict between the Soviet Union and its western neighbours and the foreign policy of extending Russian power to its western limit. Kennan suggested that not only had Russia always been an inherently aggressive state but Marxism-Leninism was now the ideological basis of Soviet aggression. A communist Soviet Union was inevitably expansionist and hostile to the West.

Kennan's telegram was well received in Washington. Secretary of State James Byrnes described it as a 'splendid analysis' and hundreds of copies were circulated within the administration. Truman also embraced Kennan's thinking. Kennan's ideas appealed to him for a number of reasons. The new president had earnestly tried to carry forward Roosevelt's policy of co-operation with the Russians, but instinctively he had always been more anti-Soviet than his predecessor. Kennan's vision of a hostile Soviet Union resonated with those anti-Soviet instincts. Even before the arrival of the Long Telegram Truman had become exasperated by the failure to settle key post-war issues with the Russians. In January 1946 he remarked that it was time to stop 'babying the Soviets'. He was also a politician who tended to view the world in black and white. His reading of Kennan's telegram was that the United States was in the right and the Soviet Union was in the wrong. Kennan's uncomplicated analysis of Soviet motives fitted with Truman's tendency to view complicated issues in simple terms. In 1945 he had been bewildered by the complexity of the problems confronting him as president and confused by Soviet behaviour. He had been searching for a clear policy towards the Russians. Kennan's argument that Soviet foreign policy was aggressive and inspired by communist ideology encouraged Truman to define the Soviet Union as an enemy and prompted a much clearer and tougher policy towards the Russians.

Changing attitudes towards the Soviet Union within the political elite were matched by a shift in the mood of the American public. Britain's wartime leader, Winston Churchill, was partly responsible for this change in public opinion. In March 1946 he gave a speech in Fulton, Missouri, which painted a menacing picture of the Soviet Union. He said that an 'iron curtain' had descended across Europe. Behind the 'iron curtain' the Soviets were building an empire in eastern Europe, beyond it they were attempting to project their power by directing communist parties in western Europe to work against elected governments. Churchill warned that the only way to deal with the Soviets was to be firm with them in negotiations. Britain and America must learn the lesson of appeasement in the 1930s. The policy of acquiescing in German territorial claims in order to avert further German aggression had failed and must not be repeated with the Russians. It was time for a new firmer policy.

Churchill's speech certainly hardened public opinion within the United States against the Soviet Union. The 'iron curtain' was a memorable phrase and a vivid metaphor for Soviet actions in eastern Europe. In June 1946 the popular illustrated magazine *Life* echoed fears about a burgeoning Soviet empire.

1 It is necessary to understand the meaning which Soviet speakers and writers give to the words 'democracy' and 'friendly'. Soviet leaders say that the goal of their foreign policy was to have everywhere democratic governments which will be friendly. That
5 seems to be reasonable until we realise that:
   'Democracy' in Russian means the Soviet type of dictatorship;
   'Friendly' in Russian is a word of approval reserved for those who profess belief in Soviet ideals.
   Soviet policy is intolerant. It seeks to eliminate what to us are the
10 essentials of a free society. It seeks this with urgency because Soviet leaders believe that, until this is done, peace is in jeopardy. Tolerance of non-Soviet thinking is, to them, weakness which is dangerous.
   Soviet leaders think that the quick way to eradicate threats is to
15 have governments everywhere which accept the political philosophy of the Soviet Union. Such governments will maintain an intensive censorship and secret police to detect those who persist in other political beliefs. By bringing such governments into power throughout the world, the Soviet Union would create world
20 harmony.

6 New Policy towards the Soviet Union

New perceptions of the Soviet Union quickly resulted in a redirection of American policy. The Americans were now practising 'patience with firmness' or a 'get tough' policy towards the Soviets, which was the forebear of the later policy of containment discussed in the next chapter. American actions in Iran signalled the new diplomatic offensive. In March 1946 Russian forces were only 40 miles from the Iranian capital Tehran and had not observed the 1 March deadline for withdrawal. The Americans took the issue to the United Nations and in May Soviet troops began to retreat. The Americans helped the Iranian army to re-establish a grip on the northern provinces of Iran. The Soviets were angry that the Americans had sought to embarrass them by raising the issue at the UN rather than attempting to negotiate a solution bilaterally. The Americans also applied a much tougher version of dollar diplomacy in loan negotiations with the Russians. They attached more stringent conditions to the loans and credits requested by the Soviets, such as the dropping of trade barriers in eastern Europe and compensation for US assets seized in Romania and Bulgaria. The Russians were not interested in US dollars on those terms and in June 1946 all negotiations over loans ended. There would be no US-Soviet economic partnership in the post-war world.

Significant changes also occurred in US occupation policy in Germany. In an attempt to secure food and commodities from the Russian zone, the Americans halted reparations deliveries to the Soviets from the western zones in May 1946. The Russians interpreted this measure as a breach of the Potsdam agreement and argued that they were being denied legitimate compensation for Soviet war losses. In July the United States and Britain agreed to merge their two zones of occupation into an area called the Bizone, which would form a single political and economic unit. The two powers were determined to implement the Potsdam agreement at least in those areas of Germany where they had control. Secretary of State James Byrnes travelled to Germany in September and announced the relaxation of restrictions on German industrial production and the creation of a central import-export agency which would enable Germany to export enough goods to finance food imports. American priorities in Germany were now clear: sustaining the German population at subsistence level and harnessing west German resources to European economic recovery were more important than satisfying Soviet reparations claims. Some US officials were even thinking in terms of the division of Germany and of tethering west Germany to western Europe in an area secure from Soviet influence. The emphasis of US occupation policy had shifted from the punishment of Germany to the rehabilitation of Germany. American actions alarmed Stalin. From his perspective it appeared that America was overseeing the economic revival of Russia's wartime enemy, and that the Bizone was the nucleus of a future west German state hostile to the Soviet Union. Privately the Soviet leader predicted, '[Germany] will recover and very quickly. Give them twelve to fifteen years and they'll be on their feet again.'

The United States also brought an uncompromising attitude to information-sharing about atomic weapons. The Americans and Russians had attempted to work out proposals for the international control of atomic weapons via the United Nations Atomic Energy Commission in 1945. The final plan presented to the UN by the Americans in June 1946, the Baruch Plan, provided for frequent inspection of atomic energy installations in UN member states. The emphasis on inspection caused an impasse between the United States and the Soviet Union. The Americans refused to destroy their existing atomic stockpile until inspection arrangements were firmly in place, while the Russian refused to submit to inspection of their sites until the Americans had destroyed their atomic weapons. Stalin might not have permitted inspection of atomic energy facilities by outside authorities in any case, since he did not want any interference with Russia's embryonic atom bomb programme, but US demands for a strict inspection regime certainly made any agreement on joint control of atomic weapons more difficult. Some historians have even argued that the Baruch Plan was explicitly designed to be unacceptable to the Russians and to prolong America's atomic monopoly. In any event the opportunity for international control of nuclear weapons was lost and Congress passed the McMahon Act (1946), prohibiting the exchange of atomic energy information with any foreign power, including America's allies. Meanwhile the Soviets pressed on with their own atom bomb project and the two sides soon found themselves in a nuclear arms race which proved to be an enduring feature of the Cold War.

During 1946 a Cold War consensus emerged within the Truman administration. There was an almost unanimous view within American government, shared by many members of Congress and the public, that the Soviet Union directly threatened the security of the United States. In July 1946 Truman commissioned two of his advisers to review US-Soviet relations, and their findings, the Clifford-Elsey Report, both reflected and crystallised the emerging Cold War consensus within US policy-making circles. The report highlighted examples of aggressive Soviet actions in Iran and Manchuria, identified ideology and not the search for security as the motor of Soviet foreign policy, argued that the Russians had constantly flouted wartime agreements, and stated that the ultimate Soviet objective was world domination. The Russians were inspired by the 'Marxian theory of ultimate destruction of capitalist states by communist states'.

Members of Truman's administration who did not share these views of the Soviet Union were marginalised. Henry Wallace, Secretary of Commerce, publicly criticised the 'Get Tough with Russia' policy in September 1946.

1 I plead for an America vigorously dedicated to peace. To achieve
  lasting peace we must study in detail how the Russian character
  was formed - by the invasion of Tartars, Mongols, Germans, Poles,
  Swedes and French; by the intervention of the British, French and
5 Americans in Russian affairs from 1919 to 1921; by the geography
  of the huge Russian land mass situated strategically between
  Europe and Asia. Add to all this the tremendous emotional power
  which Marxism and Leninism gives to the Russian leaders and

then we can realise that we are reckoning with a force which cannot
10 be handled successfully by a 'Get tough with Russia' policy. The
tougher we get, the tougher the Russians will get. We must not let
our Russian policy be guided or influenced by those inside or
outside the United States who want war with Russia. This does not
mean appeasement.

Truman's response to Wallace's public misgivings about policy towards
the Soviet Union was to sack him. Secretary of State James Byrnes was
also a political casualty. He was thought to be too lenient towards the
Russians and was replaced by George Marshall in January 1947.
Another advocate of a tough policy towards the Soviet Union, Dean
Acheson, was appointed Under-Secretary of State in 1947. The Cold
War consensus was firmly in place.

7 How Far was the United States Responsible for the Cold War?

The origins of the Cold War have been the subject of intense
historiographical debate. The Soviet Union was certainly not blameless.
The Russians did not implement the Yalta accords on Poland to the
letter, even though their actions in Poland were arguably in the spirit of
previous wartime agreements. They also blocked economic unity in
Germany. In Poland, Romania and Bulgaria they installed communist
governments and suppressed opposition parties. There is no doubt that
the Soviet Union exerted a tight hold over the east European states on its
borders. In Poland elections planned for February 1946 were postponed
and in Romania the Russians had responded to US demands for the
reorganisation of the government by adding only two opposition
politicians. In Bulgaria the pro-Soviet Fatherland Front refused to
admit any opposition members into the regime. The Russians had also
used their belated entry into the war against Japan as a pretext for
moving Soviet troops into Korea and Manchuria and exploited wartime
agreements to retain a military presence in northern Iran after the war.
Yet a common thread ran through all these actions. They all occurred on
the perimeter of the Soviet Union and were attempts by Stalin to
consolidate his frontiers. In this sense Soviet behaviour was defensive.
As it had been in the 1930s, Soviet foreign policy was largely cautious
and geared to national security.

The United States therefore frequently misinterpreted Russian
policy. It believed that the Soviet Union was systematically penetrating
areas vital to US security and was engaged in a grand design to become
the world's dominant post-war power. To this extent US policy was
based on fear. Policy-makers saw the Soviet Union as the aggressor.
They therefore took measures to underpin US security, but those
defensive measures were construed by the Russians as aggressive,

prompting the Russians to take further defensive measures which the Americans then saw as offensive. Thus a dangerous cycle of action and reaction came into being. Strategists call this situation the 'security dilemma'. The net outcome was less security for both parties.

America's misunderstanding of Soviet motives was an important cause of the Cold War. From 1946 US policy was based on the false assumption that expansionist communist ideology and not national security drove Soviet foreign policy. US officials tended to ignore evidence that did not fit with their preconceived view of a hostile Soviet Union. The Russians had not opposed the despatch of US marines to Manchuria and had eventually withdrawn their own troops from northern China. Stalin had recognised Jiang's Nationalists as the government of China and was offering only meagre assistance to the CCP. The Soviet Union had not objected to the American occupation of southern Korea, even though the area was relatively close to Soviet borders. Russian forces had also withdrawn from Iran, albeit two months after the deadline There was little hard evidence in 1945 and 1946 that Stalin wanted to dominate eastern Europe beyond Poland, Romania and Bulgaria. Democratic politics continued in Hungary and free elections took place in Czechoslovakia in May 1946. The Sovietization of eastern Europe was an effect and not a cause of the Cold War. Moreover, Soviet policy towards Greece did not suggest imminent Russian expansion into the Mediterranean. The Soviet Union did not supply weapons to the Greek communists. The Russians abided by the 1944 Moscow agreement and recognised Greece as an area of British interest. Their compliance with the Moscow agreement was contrary to the conclusion of the Clifford-Elsey report that the Soviet Union always violated international accords.

The scale of American power was also an important cause of the Cold War. The Second World War had destroyed existing balances of power within the international state system and had left the United States as the most powerful nation in the world. Germany and Japan had been reduced to unconditional surrender, while Britain and the Soviet Union had exhausted themselves in achieving victory. Arguably the United States was the only real victor at the end of the war. Relatively, US human, material and financial losses had been light. The United States had lost 0.9 per cent of its people and had not been occupied by its enemies. America had emerged from the war as an awesome economic and military superpower: it produced 50 per cent of the world's goods and services and possessed a navy of 70,000 vessels (tantamount to the rest of the world's navies put together), 100,000 planes and a monopoly of the atomic bomb. In 1945 the United States was possibly more powerful than at any other moment in the twentieth century. The Americans did not necessarily intend to intimidate the Soviet Union, but it is hardly surprising that American power provoked fear among the Russians. Russian fears of American power were more rational than

American fears of Soviet power. The Soviet Union had no long-range bombing capacity, no atomic bomb, limited air defences and an inferior navy. Stalin's one advantage lay in the size of his ground forces. At the end of the war there were six million Soviet ground troops in eastern Europe. Stalin's successor, Nikita Khrushchev, later remembered Stalin trembling when considering the prospect of war with the United States. 'How he quivered. He was afraid of war. He knew we were weaker than the United States', Khrushchev recalled.

Victory over Japan and Germany created a mood of self-confidence among Americans, a feeling that the United States could do anything. As early as 1941 the American publisher Henry Luce had described the twentieth century as the 'American century'. Walter Lippman, who coined the term 'Cold War', predicted in 1945, 'What Rome was to the ancient world, what Great Britain has been to the modern world, America is to be to the world of tomorrow.' A sense of their own power informed the plans the Americans made for the post-war world. The American programme was designed to remake the world according to US interests and in the American image. The 'one world' policy was both a self-interested and an idealistic attempt to create fresh markets for American business and to impose American values on the world. US policy-makers assumed that what was best for America was best for the remainder of the world. Naively perhaps they did not take account of Soviet interests and failed to appreciate that for example the creation of a new order of independent, democratic and capitalist states on the Soviet Union's borders could not fulfil the security needs of the Soviet Union. The global scope of the 'one world' policy also meant a much wider definition of US security interests. Areas like Poland, Manchuria and Iran, previously not of great strategic importance to the United States, were now classified as vital to US interests. Consequently the United States had to respond to threatening Soviet actions there, and American intervention in those areas only made the Soviets feel more insecure.

Recent historians of the Cold War have never suggested that the United States was solely responsible for the conflict, but their work has contributed to a more balanced view about its origins. The current consensus among historians is that both the Soviet Union and the United States bear some responsibility for the outbreak of the Cold War. The reader will have to decide how much blame to apportion to each party.

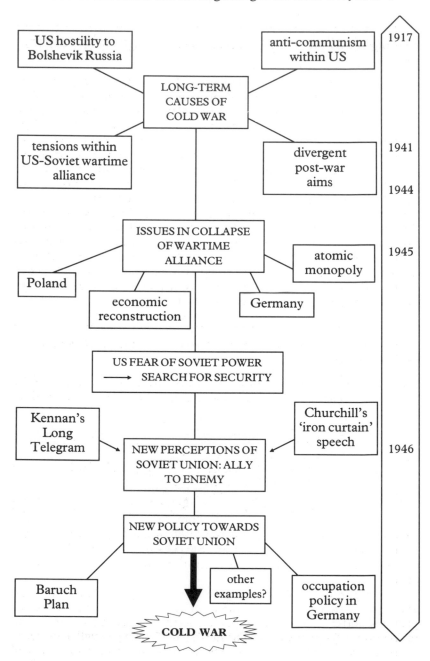

Summary - Origins: The United States and the Beginning of the Cold War, 1945-6

Making Notes on *'The United States and the Origins of the Cold War, 1945-6'*

You should have a detailed set of notes on this chapter. Your grasp of the later stages of the Cold War will depend on a clear understanding of its origins. Use the headings and the sub-headings in the chapter and the end-of-chapter summary as a backbone for your notes. You might approach the information in this chapter with questions in mind and organise your notes around answers to those questions. Here are some important issues to consider. What were the longer-term causes of the Cold War? What were the specific issues which led to the breakdown of the US-Soviet alliance in 1945? Explain how each of those issues intensified US suspicions and fears of the Soviet Union. What actions did the United States take in 1945 which indicated a growing fear of Soviet power? How and for what reasons did American views of the Soviet Union change for the worse in 1946? Think about the effect of altered perceptions of the Soviet threat on actual US policy decisions in 1946. In the final section of your notes you might try to decide the extent of US responsibility for the onset of the Cold War.

Answering essay questions on *'Origins: The United States and the Beginning of the Cold War, 1945-6'*

Here are some typical essay questions on America and the origins of the Cold War. Questions on this aspect of the Cold War will tend to concentrate on causation.

1 Explain why the United States saw the Soviet Union as an ally in 1944 but as an enemy in 1946.
2 Account for the rapid collapse of the wartime US-Soviet alliance once Nazi Germany had been defeated.
3 How far were ideological differences responsible for the growing hostility of US policy towards the Soviet Union 1944-6?

As I am sure you already appreciate, writing a history essay is a very demanding task. You are expected to produce an organised, targeted and argued response to a complex historical problem. How do you go about it?

The important planks of any good essay are a plan, an introduction and a conclusion. Time and again examiners' reports identify a lack of planning and the absence of proper introductions and conclusions as the main reasons for poor essays. The harsh truth is that you will never write a decent essay without a plan. The level of detail in your plan will depend on whether you are writing an extended or a timed essay. When you are writing against the clock, you might produce a micro-plan. Such a plan might contain a list of paragraph points, each of which is the nucleus of a paragraph in your essay. Each paragraph point is a point of argument to be developed in the paragraph and must be relevant to the question. A plan must address the question directly. Here careful reading of the question is required. In particular, search for key instruction words. They will act as a cue and determine the sort of essay you will write. You should also be looking for key terms which you might need to define in your introduction. In addition you must assess the scope of the question. Which areas of a particular topic is the question inviting you to examine, and what is the time frame of the question? The plan will act as your compass.

The purpose of the introduction is to offer clear signposts to the reader. It will advertise your approach to the question, identifying areas for discussion and analysis and defining important historical terms which appear in the question. You may wish to state the case you are going to argue in outline. The argument will then be developed in the body of your essay. The introduction gives your essay a sense of direction. Normally it will be no longer than a paragraph. What about the conclusion? For questions which require a definite opinion your conclusion will be an opportunity to deliver your judgement. For more open-ended questions you will be synthesising the different points of your essay into a coherent overview. The conclusion must leave the reader in no doubt about your line of argument or your view of a certain topic. Like the introduction, the conclusion will not normally be longer than a single paragraph.

In question 1 the instruction word is 'explain', which means that you must give reasons for the developments cited by the question. It is a question about causation. The question falls into two parts. Firstly you must identify reasons why the United States and the Soviet Union were allies in 1944. Then you have to explain why the alliance disintegrated in 1945 and why in 1946 US policy towards the Soviet Union was actually hostile. In this second part of your answer you may have to be selective and discuss only what in your view were the most important reasons for worsening US-Soviet relations. You might devote a paragraph to each reason, remembering always to establish the link between the point you are discussing and the gradual breakdown of US-Soviet relations. Question 2 belongs to the same question type as question 1. It is another question about causation. The instruction word is 'account for', which is asking you to explain the reasons for an historical event or process, indicating all relevant factors and circumstances. It is asking you to analyse the causes of the rapid collapse of the US-Soviet alliance. Your answer might fall into three parts. You might want to examine some of the longer-term reasons for the breakdown of relations, which predated the Second World War. Then you might look at strains within the wartime alliance. Thirdly you might analyse in depth the issues leading to the end of the alliance in 1945. Once again, make the link between the factors you are discussing and the deterioration of US-Soviet relations which is the subject of the question. In your conclusion you might pass judgement on which of the reasons you have discussed was the most important reason for the collapse of the US-Soviet alliance. This will give your conclusion a fresh angle and demonstrate a capacity for historical judgement.

Question 3 is of a different question type. The instruction word is 'how far'. Prompts like 'how far' or 'to what extent' are inviting you to make a case for and against. Rarely, if ever, will you be arguing 100 per cent for or 100 per cent against the suggestion made in the question, but you will be putting both sides of the argument and reaching an overall verdict in your conclusion. For example, in this particular question you may argue that ideological differences were an important reason for the rift between America and the Soviet Union. You will try to analyse how ideological conflict exacerbated tension between the two countries. On the other side, you might be arguing that there were other reasons for the start of the Cold War and explain their importance in the worsening US-Soviet relationship. This is a hard question and requires you to clarify the meaning of 'ideological differences' in your introduction. These differences encompassed contrasting value systems and different views in the United States and the Soviet Union on how the political system and the economy should be organised. As a result of those differences, the United States was suspicious of the Soviet Union long before the Cold War. Ideological differences also meant that both sides had very different post-war aims, which was an important cause of the Cold War. Different views on the importance of free elections were at the heart of the dispute over Poland. By 1946 policy-makers like Kennan thought that the Soviet Union was expansionist because it was communist. Ideology was seen as the driving force of Soviet policy. On the other hand, ideological conflict was not entirely responsible for the Cold War. Issues as well as ideas caused the Cold War. Both sides clashed on concrete issues like the atom bomb and the occupation of Germany. Also US fear of Soviet power and the US policy of establishing the United States as the dominant post-war world power were significant reasons for the Cold War. You might therefore produce a balanced, two-sided response to this question. In your conclusion you should try to assess the relative importance of ideological differences in causing the Cold War, i.e. how important were they in relation to the other factors you discussed?

Source-based questions on 'Origins: The United States and the Beginning of the Cold War, 1945-6'

1 Extracts from *Life* magazine, 1943 and 1946

Read the extracts on pages 14-15 and page 30, and answer the following questions.

a) In the context of the first extract explain the meaning of 'control of information' (line 17). (1 mark)

b) In the context of the second extract explain the meaning of 'the essentials of a free society' (line 10). (1 mark)

c) How far do the tone and language of the first extract suggest a favourable view of the Soviet Union and its people? (4 marks)

d) How useful are these two extracts as evidence of attitudes within the United States towards the Soviet Union? (6 marks)

e) Use both the sources and your own knowledge to explain the contrasting views of the Soviet Union presented in the extracts. (8 marks)

2 Henry Wallace's speech, September 1946

Read the extract from Henry Wallace's speech, given on pages 32-3, and answer the following questions.

a) In the context of the extract explain the following: i) 'intervention of the ... Americans in Russian affairs from 1919 to 1921' (lines 4-5); (2 marks) and ii) 'Get tough with Russia' policy (line 11). (2 marks)

b) How and why did President Truman react adversely to this speech? (5 marks)

c) Use your own knowledge and the extract to decide whether Wallace's criticisms of US policy towards the Soviet Union were justified. (6 marks)

CHAPTER 3

Containment: Confining Soviet Power, 1947-9

1 Introduction

In 1947 the United States adopted a policy of containment. The architect of the new policy was George Kennan, the author of the Long Telegram. The assumption underlying containment was that the Soviet Union would constantly attempt to extend its power by applying pressure on weak points beyond its own sphere of influence. It was thought that the chief instrument of Soviet expansion would not be war but communist movements in western Europe and Asia which would be directed to destabilise existing governments by methods such as propaganda and industrial strikes.

The broad objective of containment was to prevent the spread of communism beyond those areas where it already existed. In particular, it was considered essential to stop a hostile Soviet Union moving into western Europe, thereby establishing control over the Eurasian land mass and gaining access to the Atlantic seaboard. Kennan had identified five world centres of military and industrial power (the Soviet Union, the United States, Japan, Britain and the complex of coal mines and steel works in the Ruhr Valley in west Germany). Only one of these lay within the Soviet sphere of influence in 1947. It was vital to American interests to deny the resources of the other four power centres to the Russians.

Containment was not purely a defensive posture. American policy-makers calculated that the United States was more powerful than the Soviet Union. America had to exploit its position as the world's leading economy to establish a global balance of power favourable to the United States. American dollars would be used to nurture the countries of western Europe and Japan as stable, democratic and capitalist states which would form the core of a grand American area. At the same time, America would do its best to counter communism in peripheral areas such as Korea and Vietnam, though these places were always assigned a lower priority. Between 1947 and 1949 US policy-makers, confident in American power and aware of the advantages of atomic monopoly, launched a series of bold initiatives aimed at assuming leadership of the 'free world'. These initiatives included huge subsidies to western Europe in the form of the Marshall Plan, the building of a new West German state, the formation of a North Atlantic security pact and a massive infusion of dollars into Japan.

2 Truman Doctrine

Containment was first put into practice in Greece and Turkey, both of which were seen as weak points subject to Soviet pressure. Greece was in the grip of a civil war between royalists and communists, and victory for the left would draw Greece into Stalin's sphere of influence. Turkey bordered the Soviet Union and had historically been a target for Soviet expansion. Traditionally, Britain had protected the eastern Mediterranean against Russian encroachment and had continued to do so until the beginning of 1947, but in February Britain informed the United States that it could no longer afford to give financial aid to Greece and Turkey. British withdrawal left a vacuum which the United States filled. Members of the State Department argued that once the Russians drew Greece and Turkey into their orbit, they would try to extend their influence into the nearby Middle East and ultimately gain control of the region's vital oil resources. State Department officials used the analogy of the rotten apple. Just as one rotten apple eventually infected the whole barrel, so communism in Greece and Turkey would spread to neighbouring states.

Yet President Truman could not be sure that Congress would support sending American money and military advisers to Greece and Turkey. American public opinion was not yet ready for the peacetime use of American manpower and money to defend distant places. More importantly, the Republicans controlled Congress after the 1946 mid-term elections. The Republicans had stood on a popular platform of cutting taxes after the high levels of government spending during the war. Since the Democrats had occupied the White House since 1933, Republicans campaigned on the slogan, 'Had enough?' Most American voters clearly felt they had. Truman therefore had to persuade a hostile Republican Congress elected to save the American taxpayer money to allocate funds to combat communism in Greece and Turkey.

In order to unite public opinion behind the policy of containment and persuade a reluctant Congress to release the necessary funds, Truman exaggerated the threat posed by communism and dramatised the conflict between the United States and the Soviet Union as an ideological struggle between two competing sets of ideas. In a famous speech to Congress on 12 March 1947 the President announced the Truman Doctrine.

1 The very existence of the Greek state is today threatened by the terrorist activities of several thousand armed men, led by Communists, who defy the Government's authority. The Greek government is unable to cope with the situation. The Greek army
5 is small and poorly equipped. Greece must have assistance if it is to become a self-supporting and self-respecting democracy. The United States must supply that assistance. There is no other country to which Greece can turn. At the present moment in world history nearly every nation must choose between alternative ways
10 of life. The choice is too often not a free one. One way of life is

based upon the will of the majority and is distinguished by free
institutions, representative government, free elections, guarantees
of individual liberty, freedom of speech and religion and freedom
from political oppression. The second way of life is based upon the
15 will of a minority forcibly imposed upon the majority. It relies upon
terror and oppression, a controlled press and radio, fixed elections
and the suppression of personal freedoms. I believe that it must be
the policy of the United States to support free peoples who are
resisting attempted subjugation by armed minorities or by outside
20 pressures.

Truman's tactic of alarming Congress into voting for aid to Greece and
Turkey worked. Congress granted the President $400 million, of which
$250 million went to Greece and $150 million to Turkey. In fact, Stalin
remained neutral in the Greek civil war. The source of supplies to the
Greek communists was the Yugoslav leader, Tito, who was attempting
to incorporate Greece into a Balkan federation under the leadership of
Yugoslavia. Also the Greek and Turkish governments were hardly
models of democracy. They were corrupt and imprisoned and
intimidated their political opponents, exhibiting some of the very
characteristics which Truman had attributed to communism in his
speech. This was the first of many instances in the post-war period when
America was willing to support undemocratic right-wing regimes in the
fight against international communism.

3 National Security

Although military planners did not see war with the Soviet Union as a
real possibility in 1947, the announcement of the Truman Doctrine was
accompanied by an increase in military preparedness as a precautionary
measure. A system of selective service was introduced. Men of military
age were chosen by lot to serve in the armed forces alongside permanent
volunteer soldiers. Also between June 1947 and June 1948 the United
States increased its stockpile of atomic bombs - the trump card in the
event of war with the Soviet Union - from 13 to 50 and by the end of
1948 had at least 18 B-50 bombers capable of delivering the bomb.

Perhaps the most important measure taken in response to the
perceived Soviet threat was the National Security Act (1947). This was
designed to improve America's war-making capacity by merging the old
War and Navy Departments into a new enlarged Defense Department
based at the Pentagon in Washington. The Act also established the
Central Intelligence Agency (CIA) whose function was to gather
intelligence on potential enemies of the United States. The CIA was also
allowed to engage in secret operations abroad and quickly used its
powers to work against communist governments overseas. Finally, the
Act created the National Security Council (NSC) which reported

directly to the president on matters of national security. In later years the National Security Council would be a major influence in forming policy towards the Soviet Union, and its head, the National Security Adviser, would be a key figure in any presidential administration.

4 Marshall Plan

America now turned its attention to western Europe, the area of the world seen as most susceptible to Soviet influence and as the most important theatre in the Cold War. On 5 June 1947 Secretary of State George Marshall announced a massive programme of economic assistance for the countries of western Europe. It was known as the Marshall Plan and proposed large dollar grants which western European states would use to purchase food, raw materials and industrial machinery in the United States.

1 I need not tell you, gentlemen, that the world situation is very serious. The truth of the matter is that Europe's requirements for the next three or four years of foreign food and other essential products - principally from America - are so much greater than her
5 present ability to pay that she must have substantial additional help or face economic, social and political deterioration of a very grave character. The remedy lies in breaking the vicious circle and restoring the confidence of the European people in the economic future of their own countries and of Europe as a whole. Aside from
10 the demoralising effect on the world at large and the possibilities of disturbances arising as a result of the desperation of the people concerned, the consequences to the economy of the United States should be apparent to all.
  Our policy is directed not against any country or doctrine but
15 against hunger, poverty, desperation and chaos. Its purpose should be the revival of a working economy in the world so as to permit the emergence of political and social conditions in which free institutions can exist.
  Any government that is willing to assist in the task of recovery
20 will find full co-operation, I am sure, on the part of the United States government. Any government which manoeuvres to block the recovery of other countries cannot expect help from us. Furthermore, governments, political parties or groups which seek to perpetuate human misery in order to profit therefrom politically
25 will encounter the opposition of the United States.

There were various motives for the Marshall Plan. Economic motives were secondary but not unimportant. Marshall Aid would create a captive market for American goods in western Europe for the next four years and help American farmers and businessmen threatened by falling domestic demand after the end of the war. The real function of the Marshall Plan, however, was the containment of communism. In the spring of 1947 Washington's reading of the situation in western Europe was pessimistic. Americans saw a continent in the grip of economic recession. In actual fact the economy of western Europe was stronger than Americans believed, but there was some supporting evidence for their gloomy diagnosis of western Europe's condition. The severe cold of the 1946-7 winter was accompanied by coal shortages across the continent and hungry Germans had staged food riots in the western occupation zones. Americans had long believed that people who were hungry and unemployed were likely to turn to extreme parties of the left for solutions to their problems. The rise of the left in Europe was a reality. In France the Communist Party (PCF) enjoyed a membership of one million and belonged to the coalition government, while in Italy the communists had 1.7 million members. There was a real fear in Washington that the Italian communists might win the elections due in the spring of 1948. A scenario of continuing economic crisis, growing support for European communist parties followed by their electoral success and closer alignment with Moscow alarmed the United States. The Soviet Union would then control western Europe. The domination of continental Europe by a hostile totalitarian state organised around a communist ideology would threaten the national security of the United States, just as Nazi domination of Europe in 1940 had done. Consequently, a large-scale transfusion of dollars to western Europe was necessary to stimulate coal production, raise industrial output and create employment. The best antidote to communism was prosperity.

The Soviet Union and the countries of eastern Europe were invited to be part of the Marshall Plan. To rebuff Russia publicly would expose the United States to accusations of deliberately blocking co-operation with Stalin and exacerbating the Cold War. Privately, however, America hoped that Russia would turn the offer down. The countries of eastern Europe were a different matter. The United States hoped that they would accept the offer of Marshall Aid. Their participation would lessen their dependence on the Soviet Union and weaken the Soviet sphere in eastern Europe. In fact, Stalin quickly rejected the Marshall Plan and vetoed the inclusion of any states in the Soviet bloc. The Russians saw Marshall Aid as an attempt to create an American economic empire in eastern Europe. Inflows of American capital were bound to generate closer economic ties between the United States and the Soviet Union's eastern neighbours. The Americans would attempt to sell their goods there and purchase critical raw materials such as Polish coal, leaving the Soviet Union without resources and markets and economically isolated from its satellites. The disintegration of the Soviet sphere of influence would follow.

The announcement of the Marshall Plan and its rejection by Stalin was a key episode in the Cold War. It marked the moment when compromise between the two sides was no longer possible, and prompted a more aggressive Soviet policy in eastern Europe based largely on fear of the actions of the United States. The Russians produced their own version of the Marshall Plan (the Molotov Plan), which was an attempt to bind the countries of eastern Europe into a single economic area. The division of Europe into two separate economic blocs was imminent. In September 1947 Stalin reformed the Comintern, now renamed the Cominform (the Communist Information Bureau). Its functions were to circulate propaganda abroad, liaise with the communist parties of western Europe and assist their attempts to obstruct elected governments. The PCF was instructed to frustrate the Marshall Plan by asking its members in the French trade union movement to foment strikes. A wave of industrial unrest hit France at the end of 1947. At the same time Stalin consolidated his position in eastern Europe. Hitherto he had accepted a degree of free enterprise and democratic politics in countries such as Hungary, but at the beginning of 1948 non-communists were expelled from the Hungarian government and Stalinists were placed in key positions. Events in Czechoslovakia were the best example of Stalin's tightening grip on the Soviet bloc. When the Czechs pursued their interest in the Marshall Plan, the Czech communists seized power in February 1948 and the pro-western Czech foreign minister, Jan Masaryk, was murdered.

Marshall Aid went ahead in western Europe. Opposition in Congress to financial aid on such a large scale crumbled in the aftermath of the Czech coup and in the same month Congress granted the President $17 billion which was to be distributed to the participating countries over a period of four years through the Economic Co-operation Administration (ECA). Between 1948 and 1952 total Marshall Aid spending amounted to $13 billion. The major recipients were the motor economies of Europe: Britain, France and Germany. By 1952 industrial production had increased by 35 per cent over pre-war levels and agricultural output by 10 per cent. There is no doubt that the economic recovery of post-war western Europe was greatly accelerated by Marshall Aid.

5 Creation of a West German State

The rise of Russian power in the east persuaded the United States to revive Germany more quickly than had been planned at the Potsdam Conference. The location of western Germany at the junction between non-communist Europe and occupied eastern Europe made it a vital battleground in the Cold War. America took the lead in arguing for an early end to military occupation and the combination of the three western occupation zones into a west German state, which would become an American ally and a solid buffer against communism in central Europe. The alternative prospect of a single Soviet-dominated

German state was alarming. It would give Russia control over the coalfields and heavy industries of the Ruhr and bring Soviet domination of the Eurasian land-mass one step closer. According to the strategy of containment, western Germany was seen as a prime site of Soviet pressure. American counter-pressure partly took the form of Marshall Aid dollars. West Germany was one of the chief beneficiaries of the Marshall Plan, as the ECA channelled millions of dollars into the western zones.

America's principal concern was that the Germans in the west would want to join those in the Soviet zone in a unified Germany under Soviet control. The United States believed that it was engaged in a battle with the Soviet Union for German public opinion. Accordingly, a number of steps were taken to win the support of the west German people. In 1947 restrictions on industrial production were relaxed. This measure was designed to increase the supply of west German coal and steel needed to rebuild the economy of western Europe, but it was also intended to remind the Germans that the occupiers did not want harsh external controls over German everyday life to remain in place indefinitely. The day-to-day running of west Germany was increasingly shared between the occupying powers and Germans themselves, and west Germans were promised a state of their own. In 1948 the three occupying powers met to draw up a constitution for a new west German state, which would come into existence the following year. The long-term American policy of creating a democratic and economically healthy west Germany to fortify western Europe's border with the Soviet sphere was close to fruition. American policy makers hoped that such a state might even act as a magnet to Germans in the Soviet zone leading to the emergence of a single Germany lying wholly outside the Soviet bloc.

One important measure prior to setting up a new west German state was the introduction of a new currency in the three western zones in June 1948. The old German currency had lost its value and in many areas Germans were operating a barter economy. Stalin rightly interpreted the creation of a single currency as the signal for the establishment of a new Germany in the west. The Russians were horrified at the prospect of the recovery of the west German economy and possible German rearmament, which had been forbidden under the Potsdam agreements. The spectre of an economically strong and rearmed Germany revived fears of an invasion from the west and a third world war. Stalin's response was to initiate a land blockade of Berlin. He realised that Berlin was the most vulnerable point at which he could apply pressure on the western powers. At the Potsdam Conference the city had been divided between the four occupying powers. The problem for the three western powers was that the former German capital lay deep within the Soviet occupation zone, which had been sealed off from the rest of Germany since 1946. American, French and British forces in west Berlin and west Berliners therefore depended on the western zones for vital supplies which were delivered along road, rail and land corridors.

In June 1948 Russia blocked the road and rail routes to Berlin. The purpose of the blockade was to force the United States, Britain and France to cancel their plans for a west German state. Failing that, the Russians could at least drive the western powers out of Berlin. Truman was determined to stay in Berlin without going to war with the Russians. The tactic adopted was to supply west Berlin from the air. During the resulting Berlin Airlift American and British planes flew more than 200,000 flights to Berlin in 320 days and delivered vital supplies of food and coal to 2.2 million west Berliners. In May 1949 Stalin ended the blockade. The blockade had been defeated by the remarkable logistical feat of the airlift and the Soviet Union had been unable to delay the American policy of creating a west German state within the US orbit.

The Berlin Airlift was the first crisis of the Cold War in Europe and a major victory for the Americans. The United States was determined to resist Soviet pressure in Berlin. Americans believed that the evacuation of Berlin would have been a sign of weakness to the Russians and encouraged them to apply pressure elsewhere in Europe. Withdrawal from Berlin would also have depressed the morale of west Germans. It was important to reassure west Germans that America could protect them from Russia. Otherwise Germans in the west might have looked east for protection and accepted a single German state within the Soviet sphere.

The end of the blockade was followed closely by free elections to choose the first West German government and the birth of the Federal Republic of Germany in September 1949. The new West Germany was not yet allowed an army, and American, British and French forces remained on German soil as a safeguard against German aggression, as well as against an invasion of western Europe by Soviet land forces. In October 1949 the Soviet occupation zone became the German Democratic Republic . Stalin's hand had been forced by the Americans. He had to give east Germans a state of their own in order to retain their support. However, the new East Germany was firmly within the Soviet sphere. It was a one-party state governed by the reconstituted German Communist Party, the SED, and large numbers of Russian troops were stationed there. The partition of Germany reflected the division of Europe as a whole. The Cold War meant that neither superpower could allow the whole of Germany to fall within the other's sphere of influence. Both the United States and Russia therefore decided that having half of Germany was better than having none.

6 North Atlantic Treaty Organisation (1949)

In April 1949 the evolving American sphere of influence in western Europe was further consolidated when the United States signed the

Divided Europe in 1949

treaty which established the North Atlantic Treaty Organisation (NATO). This was a historic moment in the foreign policy of the American republic. It was the first treaty signed with a European state since the Americans had concluded an alliance with France in 1778 to drive the British out of the 13 colonies. NATO was a military alliance of 12 states (United States, Canada, Britain, France, Belgium, Netherlands, Luxembourg, Italy, Portugal, Denmark, Norway and Iceland), which adopted the principle of collective security whereby an attack on one or more member states would be considered an attack on them all and could be met with armed force (Article 5).

It has been said that NATO was created 'to keep the Russians out, the Germans down and the Americans in'. There is some truth in this. Both Britain and France realised that the defence of western Europe was only viable with American participation. They wanted a permanent US military presence on the continent as a guarantee against Soviet attack. In the case of France NATO would also be a useful shield against a resurgent Germany. Even as late as 1949 French fear of Germany was acute and the priority of French policy was not so much the containment of the Soviet Union as the taming of Germany. Prior to 1949 the United States had shown no great interest in garrisoning US troops permanently on the continent. The focus of American policy in western Europe had been economic and political reconstruction. The Americans had encouraged their European allies to form their own defence organisation in 1948, the Western European Union (WEU), but saw no need for their own participation. A Soviet invasion of western Europe was never regarded as a real possibility in this period.

The United States joined NATO firstly for political and secondly for military reasons. It became clear to Washington that American membership of a security pact was a precondition of French and, to a lesser extent, British consent to west German statehood. In addition, the creation of NATO tied a relatively strong Britain more closely to a still recovering western Europe, calmed French security fears, and offered anxious Germans protection against the Soviet Union. NATO membership brought several military advantages to the United States too: evasion of sole responsibility for the defence of Europe in the unlikely event of Soviet invasion, valuable bases from which air attacks against the Soviet Union could be launched, and a framework for an eventual west German contribution to European defence.

7 US Policy towards Asia

The focus of the policy of containment was western Europe. This was the area identified as most vulnerable to Soviet interference, and the lion's share of US economic aid was channelled to Britain and the continental states. The United States deliberately pursued a Europe-first policy. Yet policy-makers also feared the projection of Soviet influence into Asia. The threat inherent in Soviet communism was perceived as worldwide and the scope of America's response was correspondingly global. America therefore employed the strategy of containment in Asia, albeit on a more limited scale than in Europe. The principal means of containment were: the conversion of Japan into a satellite of the United States; substantial financial assistance to anti-communist forces in China and Vietnam; support for an independent non-communist South Korea; and war plans to defend a crescent of offshore Pacific islands against an aggressor (most probably the Soviet Union) - the so-called defensive perimeter strategy.

a) Japan

After unconditional surrender in August 1945 Japan was subjected to military occupation by American forces under the command of General Douglas MacArthur. A four-power Allied Council for Japan was set up, which included the Soviet Union, but on the ground real power lay with the Americans and the United States was the sole occupying power. Soviet requests to occupy a zone of their own had been firmly refused.

Between 1945 and 1947 the main objectives of occupation policy were demilitarisation and democratisation. The Japanese armed forces were demobilised, stockpiles of weapons were destroyed and a 'no war' clause (Article Nine) was written into a new Japanese constitution in 1946. Some of Japan's vast industrial combines (zaibatsus) were broken up in order to neutralise Japan's war-making capacity. The right to strike was recognised and trade unions were legalised, as were a range of political parties, including the Japanese Communist Party. There were also punitive aspects to the American occupation: war criminals were brought to trial and Japan was forced to pay reparations to its former enemies in the Pacific war.

However, the onset of the Cold War and American concern about the growing influence of the Soviet Union in Asia altered the direction of American policy from 1947. Of all the countries in Asia Japan was considered the most important to US national security. Controlling Japan held the key to the balance of power in Asia. On account of its concentration of skilled labour and industrial plant Japan represented one of the five military-industrial world power centres which must remain within the American orbit. From 1947 the goal of American policy was therefore to deny Japan to the Soviet Union. Securing Japan as an ally firmly anchored to the United States was the cornerstone of the strategy of containment in Asia.

Yet American plans for Japan were jeopardised by the economic situation there. The war had resulted in serious losses in property and human life. Two and a half million Japanese citizens had died and in Japan's 66 largest cities 40 per cent of the buildings had been destroyed. Agricultural and industrial output was low, prices were soaring and

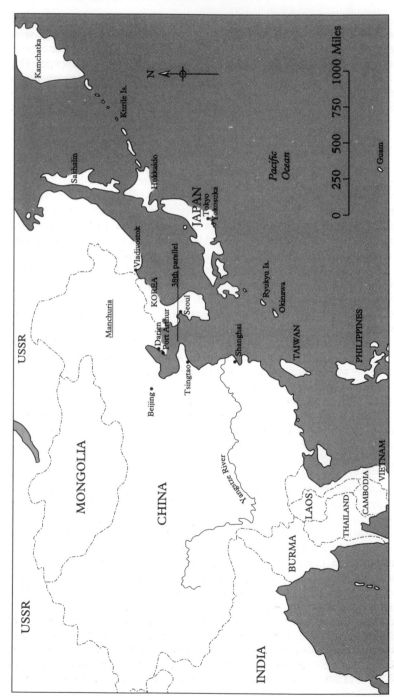

The Far East in 1947

unemployment was widespread. As in Germany, Americans worried about the allure of communism to a defeated and demoralised people. There were some grounds for such fears. The Communist Party, encouraged by the Soviet mission in Tokyo, was gaining support. The year 1949 opened with a series of industrial strikes and the Japanese communists polled three million votes in elections. The rise of the left raised the spectre of the communisation of Japan not from without as the result of Soviet military action, but from within.

Again, as in western Europe, Americans believed that the best way to counter communism was to remove the economic conditions which created it. The emphasis of occupation policy from 1947 fell heavily upon economic reconstruction. The programme of industrial deconcentration was diluted and restrictions on industrial production were relaxed so as not to hinder economic recovery. In 1948 government workers were forbidden to strike and US occupation authorities started arresting communist sympathisers in the Japanese trade union movement. Moreover, in 1949 Congress authorised $500 million in aid to Japan to allow the purchase of foodstuffs and raw materials essential to Japanese economic growth.

The whole American occupation became less harsh in an attempt to buy the support of the Japanese people. The United States was conscious that tight occupation controls might erode goodwill towards the Americans and drive the Japanese into the arms of the Soviet Union. Consequently the prosecution of war criminals was quietly scaled down, responsibility for day-to-day government was increasingly handed over to the Japanese, Japanese police forces were strengthened and plans were laid for an eventual end to occupation and a non-punitive peace treaty. The course of US policy had been set and the work of cementing Japan's place in the American orbit begun.

b) China

Attempts by the United States in China to bolster Jiang Jieshi and erode the influence of the Chinese communists had met with little success in 1946. Jiang was an exasperating ally: he was vain, corrupt, dictatorial and his skills as a battlefield commander were limited. Marshall wanted Jiang to come to terms with the communists while he enjoyed the upper hand in the civil war so that the KMT's superiority would be reflected in majority status in a peacetime government. Jiang instead insisted that the CCP could be defeated on the battlefield. Marshall, himself a military man, realised that total victory in the civil war was impossible and feared that a continued civil war would only encourage the Soviet Union to interfere in China and openly support the CCP. By the end of 1946 relations between Marshall and Jiang were close to breaking point and Marshall recommended terminating aid to America's long-standing ally altogether. He likened helping Jiang to 'pouring sand down a rat-hole'. Contributions to Jiang were sharply reduced.

Yet Washington's new view of the world and Soviet intentions in 1947 quickly resulted in the resumption of substantial aid even to an ally as unreliable as Jiang. In spite of barely any assistance from Moscow, the CCP had been making gains in the civil war. America now feared either direct or indirect Soviet control over a complex of raw material sources and industrial sites in north-east Asia. Russian troops already occupied northern Korea and now the CCP had established a grip on Manchuria and northern China, areas with extensive iron ore and coal reserves. Prior to the Second World War Japan had seized areas which were densely populated and industrialised or rich in natural resources in an attempt to guarantee raw material supplies and markets for Japanese products. What was in effect a Japanese empire in the Far East had been euphemistically called the East Asia Co-Prosperity Sphere. America had not fought the Pacific War to see a similar area in the Far East created under the aegis of the Soviet Union. For the United States the Cold War was as much a conflict over the control of key resources as a battle of ideas. US assistance to Jiang should nevertheless be placed in context. American aid to the Nationalists was still relatively modest and did not compare to the sums expended by the United States on rehabilitating Japan. Washington always saw Japan as a higher priority than China. In 1947 American policy in China revolved around rescuing the country from communism, while at the same time not squandering precious dollars on an unpredictable ally.

American policy soon had to adjust to the new balance of power emerging in China. The successful communist offensive of 1947 was followed by further battlefield victories in 1948. The Nationalists were now losing the civil war. The American objective was no longer to achieve Nationalist control of the entire Chinese mainland, but to pen the CCP into northern China and avert communist control of central and southern China. Nationalist domination of at least these areas was an essential aspect of American strategy in the Far East. The recovery of Japan depended on access to the resources and markets of the Chinese interior. Americans assumed that a communist China would block the export of raw materials needed by Japan's industrial economy and close its markets to Japanese goods. American aid to the Nationalists continued but the surrender of Jiang's commander in the Beijing region in early 1949 heralded the collapse of the Nationalist war effort. Communist victory was now only a matter of time. Mao's forces would soon cross the Yangtze River and dominate China.

c) Korea, Vietnam and the Defensive Perimeter

The Americans had envisaged the partition of Korea into two occupation zones as a temporary arrangement. Their long-term aim was to unify Korea under a government chosen by free and fair elections, but worsening Soviet-American relations meant that neither side could agree on terms for elections and unification. The state of the Cold War in 1947 convinced policy-makers that America must hold on to South Korea at least. Even though Korea did not belong to the core of states deemed vital to US national security, communism must be contained on the Asian periphery. Washington was already concerned about the advance of communism in neighbouring Manchuria and the indirect control Moscow exercised via Kim over northern Korea with its extensive hydro-electric power capacity. Moreover, Soviet domination of the entire Korean peninsula would deprive recovering Japan of an important trading partner.

In the absence of Soviet-American agreement on unification two separate Korean states emerged in 1948: the Democratic People's Republic of Korea was created in the north, and the Republic of Korea in the south. In August 1948 elections were held in the south and Syngman Rhee was confirmed as leader. Soviet troops left the north in 1948, but Moscow remained on friendly terms with Kim and supplied him with T-34 tanks. A small detachment of US troops remained in the south until 1949 but then departed. The United States continued to send economic aid to Syngman Rhee but did not want a permanent military presence in South Korea. The Europe-first policy precluded substantial assistance to Rhee's regime and Truman was in any case concerned that American soldiers might become entangled in the ongoing civil war between north and south. Both Syngman Rhee and Kim Il Sung were intent on reunifying the Korean peninsula by force and 100,000 Koreans had died in skirmishes and intermittent hostilities between north and south since 1945.

Like Korea, Vietnam had been occupied by the Japanese during the war. Previously Vietnam had been part of the French empire in Indochina (Vietnam, Laos and Cambodia). Subjection to a European colonial power and then wartime occupation by Japan had stimulated nationalism in Vietnam and an appetite for independence. The leader of the Vietnamese nationalists was a communist called Ho Chi Minh and the movement he led was the Vietminh. In 1945 the United States had applied pressure on France to grant independence to its former colonies in Indochina. After all, one of Roosevelt's aims for the post-war era had been decolonisation - the dissolution of the overseas empires of the major European powers. Ho even approached Washington unsuccessfully for aid. However, the outbreak of hostilities between the French and the communist Vietminh in 1946 led the Americans to side firmly with France against Ho. At the same time, the United States urged France to make concessions to non-communist nationalists within Vietnam and prepare the country gradually for self-government. The Vietminh would thus be outflanked and an independent Vietnamese state under communist rule and oriented to Moscow would be avoided.

In 1949 Vietnam was offered a limited form of independence by the

French: a native government was appointed under Bao Dai, but France retained control of defence and foreign policy. Token independence was not enough for the Vietminh and they continued their war against the French. Both China and the Soviet Union recognised the Vietminh as the official government of Vietnam in 1950. The United States responded by formally opening diplomatic relations with Bao Dai. Meanwhile, opinion in Washington towards Ho Chi Minh had hardened. Secretary of State Acheson labelled him an 'outright commie' and members of the State Department assumed that he was directed from Moscow. In March 1950 there was a significant turn in American policy. Military aid was sent to the French for the first time in the hope that they could defeat the Vietminh on the battlefield. Ho was now seen as a major threat to America interests in Asia. The withdrawal of the French from Vietnam would swell the rising tide of communism in Asia and encourage Chinese communists fighting the British in Malaya. The loss of Vietnam might also turn public opinion against the French government at home, possibly to the benefit of the French communists. American support for France in Indochina was in fact closely related to US policy goals in Europe. Military aid to France was partly designed to buy French approval for the renaissance of German economic and military power central to US strategy in western Europe.

While the United States was prepared to grant dollars to the French and the Chinese Nationalists enabling them to procure the military hardware and supplies necessary to defeat communism, the deployment of US troops on the Asian mainland was never contemplated at this time. This did not mean that the Asian rim was unimportant. A key objective of US policy was to unite the Asian periphery and the Japanese core into a single self-supporting economic area. However, communism on the Asian periphery would be countered not by a policy of direct military intervention but by a policy of economic aid to existing anti-communist forces. The first line of military defence against communism in Asia would not be the land mass but a belt of offshore islands including Japan, the Ryukyu Islands, Guam and the Philippines, which roughly formed an inverted U-shape. US air bases and garrisons existed on all these islands and formed a so-called defence perimeter against an Asian aggressor. The experience of the Second World War had taught the United States the dangers of ceding control of the Pacific to an enemy state. The actual enemy then had been Japan; the potential enemy now was the Soviet Union.

8 How Successful was the Policy of Containment?

Measured by its own objectives the policy of containment had met with reasonable success in Europe by September 1949. America's policy of risk-taking had helped to produce in western Europe a collection of states friendly to the United States with multi-party political systems and free market economies. The influx of American dollars was partially responsible for gradually increasing levels of output, employment and trade, and slowly improving living standards. It seemed that the conditions which bred political extremism were receding. Within western Europe America had also begun the political and economic rebuilding of the area most open to Soviet encroachment, western Germany. Marshall Aid had acted as a catalyst to economic recovery there, and in the second half of 1949 industrial production doubled. In August 1949 the Christian Democrats won free elections and Konrad Adenauer became the first Chancellor of the new Federal Republic of Germany. The United States had served as midwife to the birth of a democratic and economically stable west German state on the frontier with the eastern bloc. By 1949 most of the countries of northern and western Europe were also organised into an anti-Soviet defensive pact under American leadership, NATO. All in all, Russian control of the western part of the Eurasian land mass with its concentration of heavy industry and mineral resources had been averted. The Soviet Union had been denied an outlet to the Atlantic Ocean, whose domination by the United States was vital to national security according to the US military.

Territorially, communism had made no gains. The one obvious attempt at Soviet expansion had been defeated by the Berlin Airlift. In Greece the KKE had been defeated in the civil war as a result of a combination of American aid, Stalin's neutrality and Tito's decision in 1948 to stop supplying the Greek communists with weapons. The influence of communist parties within western Europe was also in decline. This was not always the direct result of American actions but nevertheless fulfilled American policy objectives. In France the PCF had left the cabinet in May 1947 after a squabble with their coalition partners. Their decision later in 1947 to obey Moscow and block the Marshall Plan left them politically isolated from mainstream political parties keen to receive US dollars to rebuild the French economy. In the 1948 Italian elections the communists were defeated by the conservative Christian Democrats. The CIA had contributed financially to the Christian Democrat campaign and circulated anti-communist propaganda, but it has been shown that the Christian Democrats would have won even without CIA intervention.

In Asia the strategy of containment had been less effective. One obvious success had been Japan. By 1949 the work of political and economic reconstruction was well under way and post-war Japan was emerging as a US satellite and bulwark against communist expansion in the Far East. In Korea the Americans had managed to exclude communism from at least the southern part of the peninsula and had overseen the creation of an independent non-communist state in the south. Yet the new Republic of Korea was a more fragile entity than the new West Germany. It was vulnerable to incursions from the north and Kim Il Sung's ambition to unite the two Koreas under communist rule.

US policy in China had been an outright failure. The Nationalists had received $3 billion since 1945, yet had lost the civil war. Jiang had proved a mercurial and ultimately ineffective ally. The establishment of the People's Republic of China in 1949 was undoubtedly a major advance for international communism. American policy towards Vietnam had also met with little success. Bao Dai was an unpopular figurehead and, in spite of American aid, French troops were making little headway against the guerrilla forces of the Vietminh.

There were many reasons why containment was less successful in Asia than in Europe, but two particular points are worth thinking about. Policy-makers never committed the same resources or attached the same importance to restricting communism in Asia. American policy was resolutely Europe-first. Secondly, the communist threat was more complex in Asia than in Europe. Americans were slow to appreciate the diversity of Asian communism. Communist forces everywhere were assumed to be part of a monolithic movement answerable to Moscow. In fact, many Asian communist groups had only remote links with the Soviet Union and commanded support because of purely local circumstances. The popularity of leaders like Mao Zedong and Ho Chi Minh was a function not of their association with Moscow but of internal revolutions in China and Vietnam. Even if the United States had devoted more resources to the war against Mao and increased aid to the French in Indochina, it is questionable whether the CCP and the Vietminh would have been defeated. There was certainly a groundswell of support for the left in post-war Europe, but no European communist party had a comparable power base to the CCP. In Vietnam the Vietminh did not enjoy the same backing as the CCP in China, but Ho was still riding a tide of nationalism generated by years of French colonialism and wartime Japanese occupation. In an attempt to suppress communism in Vietnam, the United States was siding with an unpopular colonial power against a champion of national independence.

The containment of communism in western Europe can be explained by the massive diversion of American resources to the nations of the region, the fact that the communist threat was never as serious as the Americans supposed, and the defeat of communist parties in free elections which in any case reflected limited sympathy with communist politics among west European voters. In parts of Asia, however, communism and revolutionary nationalism cross-fertilised to create large and well-supported movements. The relative failure to contain communism in many regions of Asia was the consequence more of the inherent popularity of communism based on circumstances the United States could not control than of a lack of American resources and willpower.

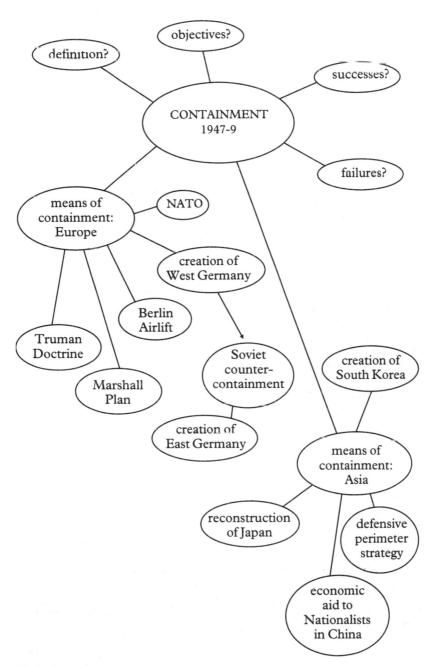

Summary - Containment: Confining Soviet Power, 1947-9

Making Notes on 'Containment: Confining Soviet power 1947-9'

Use the end-of-chapter summary and the chapter headings as the basis for your notes. In the opening section of your notes you should try to define the term 'containment'. Then examine the objectives of containment. When noting the rest of the chapter, bear the following questions in mind. What was the Truman Doctrine? What measures did the US take in 1947 to enhance national security and counter communism more effectively? What were the goals of the Marshall Plan and what form did Marshall Aid take? Why has the Marshall Plan been seen as a decisive moment in the Cold War? Why did the US mount the Berlin Airlift in 1948? How and why did the US oversee the creation of a west German state in 1949? Why did the US join NATO and what was the role of NATO in countering the Soviet threat?

You should deal with Asia in a separate section of your notes. Once again it might be a good idea to organise your notes around answers to a series of questions. Within Asia, why did the US think it was vital to exclude communism from Japan? By what means did the US begin the political and economic rehabilitation of Japan? How did the US attempt to contain communism in China between 1947 and 1949? What were the goals and methods of US policy in Korea and Vietnam in this period? What was the defensive perimeter strategy? Finally, you might wish to draw up some sort of balance sheet, itemising the successes and failures of the policy of containment in this period. To do this, it is helpful to measure policy outcomes against policy goals. Again, it will be useful to make a distinction between Europe and Asia.

Answering essay questions on 'Containment: Confining Soviet Power 1947-9'

Typical essay questions on this phase of the Cold War might be:

1   To what extent was the United States successful in containing communism in western Europe 1947-9?
2   By what means and with what success did the United States counter the expansion of communism in Western Europe?
3   Why was the United States more successful in containing communism in Western Europe than in Asia 1947-9?

For question 1 you should try to define the subject matter and scope of the question. The question is about the strategy of containment in a particular region, western Europe, during the period 1947-9. The instruction phrase is 'to what extent'. 'To what extent' or 'how far' invites you to make a case for and a case against. Having put a case for and a case against you will have to reach some sort of verdict in your conclusion. How might we apply this approach to question 1? You could argue that the US policy of containment in western Europe was a total success or a total failure, but this would be a mistake. The only defensible approach is to argue that the policy scored some successes and some failures. The first part of the essay might examine the successes and the second part the failures. Your conclusion should then judge the overall effectiveness of the policy of containment in western Europe. Question 2 is a similar question, but with one important difference. The first part of the question asks you to examine the methods of containment. In this more straightforward part of the essay you will describe how the policy of containment was implemented. Question 3 is a different category of question. Our prompt word is 'why'. It is therefore a 'reasons for' question complicated by an element of contrast. In order to explain why containment was more effective in Europe than in Asia, think about the priorities assigned to the two regions by US policy-makers, the resources allocated to the two regions by the United States, and external circumstances. On the last point you might want to think about the different nature of the communist threat in Asia.

Source-based questions on 'Containment: Confining Soviet Power 1947-9'

1 Truman Doctrine, 1946
Read the extract on pages 42-3 and answer the following questions.
a) On what grounds does Truman argue that the United States should extend economic aid to Greece? (2 marks)
b) How reliable is Truman's speech as evidence of the actual political situation in Greece at the time? (4 marks)
c) How useful is this extract to a historian studying the US policy of containment? (4 marks)

2 Marshall Plan, 1947
Read the extract on page 44 and answer the following questions.
a) In the context of the extract explain the following: i) 'revival of a working economy' (line 16); (2 marks) ii) 'political parties or groups which seek to perpetuate human misery' (lines 23-4). (2 marks)
b) 'Our policy is directed not against any country or doctrine but against hunger, poverty, desperation and chaos.' Use both the extract and your own knowledge to explain how far this is a satisfactory explanation of the motives of the Marshall Plan. (6 marks)

CHAPTER 4

Escalation: Global Cold War, Hot War in Korea, 1949-53

1 New Communist Threats

In the autumn of 1949 the objectives of US policy were the same as they had been since 1947. The United States wanted to reinforce the core of the free world (western Europe and Japan), while limiting the advance of communism on the periphery, especially Asia. In all areas Soviet power and influence must be curtailed. According to US analysts the survival of the Soviet Union depended on continued opportunities for expansion. Deprived of such opportunities the whole Soviet system would collapse in upon itself and America would win the Cold War. Yet two events rapidly transformed the situation and ushered in a new and dangerous phase of the Cold War.

The first of these events, CCP victory in the Chinese civil war, was expected. In October 1949 the Nationalists had quit the Chinese mainland and retreated to the off-shore island of Taiwan. The People's Republic of China was formed and Mao invited foreign governments to establish diplomatic relations with the new China. Mao's victory was a disaster for the United States. A vast new communist state now existed in Asia. The Americans suspected that the Chinese communists were agents of the Kremlin and that Stalin would exploit his friendship with Mao to promote communism in Indochina and south-east Asia. The defeat of the Nationalists was widely described in the United States as the 'fall' of China. China had been lost to communism and the continent of Asia now lay exposed to the communist menace.

Although relations between the Kremlin and the CCP had often been frosty, Stalin regarded Mao's victory as a momentous event and moved quickly to cement an alliance with the People's Republic. He hoped that the CCP would promote Soviet interests in Asia, and was prepared to concede China a role as a regional power in Asia, provided China in return respected its border with the Soviet Union and toed the Soviet line towards the United States. In February 1950 the two sides signed a 30-year mutual assistance treaty under which the Soviet Union promised to provide China with $300 million in credits.

The response of the United States to the formation of the People's Republic was indecisive. The United States refused to open diplomatic relations with the new regime, but at the same time withdrew aid from Jiang Jieshi. No explicit promise was made to help him defend Taiwan against an expected communist invasion. In his own words Secretary of State Acheson was waiting 'for the dust to settle'. He contemplated a wedge strategy which would divide Moscow and Beijing and pre-empt a dangerous amalgamation of Soviet and Chinese power. In spite of personal hostility towards the CCP, Acheson wanted to be on reasonable terms with Mao Zedong in the interests of the United States. He even considered recognition of China in an attempt to detach the CCP from their supposed masters in Moscow. Even after the Sino-Soviet Treaty of 1950, Acheson had not given up hope of wooing Mao. Ultimately, however, the United States proved unable to influence events on the Chinese mainland. In the short term, at least, Mao had sided with the Soviet Union. Also the Republicans in Congress would never have allowed the Truman administration to open relations with communist China.

A month before the 'fall' of China US intelligence sources had detected traces of radioactivity in the northern Pacific. The Soviet Union had detonated its first atomic bomb. The news caused panic in Washington. The United States had not expected the Soviets to develop an atomic capability until mid-1950 or 1951. It turned out that the Americans had underestimated the technological expertise of the Russians. In addition information supplied by the Soviet spy Klaus Fuchs, who had worked on the Manhattan Project, had enabled the Russians to develop a weapon which was virtually a replica of the first US bomb. Soviet possession of the bomb had major consequences. Acheson commented that it 'changed everything'. The American atomic monopoly was over. The monopoly had been militarily and diplomatically valuable to the United States. It had provided a shield behind which America pursued its risk-taking policy of building positions of strength outside the Soviet sphere and had acted as a deterrent against an invasion of western Europe by the numerically superior Soviet land armies. US war plans were based on strategic bombing of the Soviet Union with atomic weapons and America had amassed a stockpile of 50 atomic bombs. One immediate consequence of the end of the US atomic monopoly was Truman's authorisation in January 1950 of a programme to develop a thermonuclear or hydrogen bomb based not on fission but on the fusion process. If monopoly was no longer possible, at least the United States could enjoy superiority in the field of nuclear weapons.

2 NSC 68

The events of 1949 forced the Truman administration to review both the goals and the tactics of American policy towards the Soviet Union. Political pressure from the Republicans also made such a review necessary. Truman's unexpected triumph in the presidential election of 1948 was a fifth consecutive victory for the Democrats and a major setback for the Republicans. Party politics grew increasingly bitter. In particular, the Republicans attempted to discredit Truman's foreign policy by claiming that it was not tough enough on communism. The Democrats were blamed for the 'loss' of China, and one Republican senator, Joe McCarthy, even alleged that there were closet communists in the State Department (see Chapter 7). In short, the Truman administration could not be seen to be inactive in response to the 'fall' of China and Soviet possession of the atomic bomb.

The outcome of the reappraisal of policy was NSC 68, a document produced by the National Security Council in April 1950. NSC 68 demonstrated the underlying continuity of American policy. Its definition of the Soviet threat differed little from Kennan's in the Long Telegram.

1 The Soviet Union is animated by a new fanatic faith antithetical to our own and seeks to impose its absolute authority over the rest of the world. Being a totalitarian dictatorship, the Kremlin's objective in these policies is the total subjective submission of the peoples
5 now under its control. The concentration camp is the prototype of the society which these policies are designed to achieve, a society in which the personality of the individual is so broken and perverted that he participates in his own degradation. The Kremlin is inescapably militant because it possesses a world-wide revolution-
10 ary movement and because it is a totalitarian dictatorship. It is quite clear from Soviet theory and practice that the Kremlin seeks to bring the free world under its domination by the methods of the war.

NSC 68 also exemplified the consistency of the objectives of US diplomacy: the confining of communism to those areas where it already existed, then the gradual erosion of Soviet influence and power within the Soviet sphere and ultimately the downfall and transformation of the Soviet system itself. The achievement of these aims depended on the continuing ascendancy of the United States within the international state system. American policy was based on a simple calculation: the United States must remain more powerful than the Soviet Union in order to win the Cold War. The key to a global balance of power favourable to the United States was to draw the power centres of Japan, the workshop of Asia, and industrialised western Europe into the American orbit.

Yet NSC 68 marked a departure from existing policy in one important respect. Previously America had relied upon its position as the world's dominant economy to wage the Cold War, channelling dollars to strategically vital areas. America's armed forces had remained relatively small. Now NSC 68 proposed a substantial increase in military strength. The United States must expand both its conventional forces and its arsenal of atomic weapons and accelerate development of a hydrogen bomb. In this sense NSC 68 was a clear response to the passing of the atomic monopoly. Soviet access to the bomb might encourage the Soviet Union to pursue a more aggressive policy and shift the balance of power between the United States and Russia. The Russians might even threaten to use atomic weapons to block American initiatives. US officials believed that American successes prior to 1950 had been based on American dominance. The bomb had been the basis of US superiority and permitted an adventurous policy of building an American sphere of influence without the risk of Soviet reprisals. Now the only means of maintaining America's relative advantage over the Soviet Union and building on earlier successes was a massive military build-up.

In April 1950 NSC 68 existed only as a set of proposals. Truman broadly agreed with its analysis of Soviet policy and its conclusions, but knew that an enlargement of America's armed forces would require higher taxes and possibly cuts in welfare programmes. Both would be politically unpopular. There was also no history in the United States of large armies in peacetime. Truman's immediate reaction to NSC 68 was to do nothing. In the end, events forced his hand. While he was contemplating NSC 68, North Korean forces were massing north of the 38th parallel. The Korean War was about to erupt and within two years almost every recommendation made in NSC 68 had been implemented.

3 Turning Point: War in Korea, 1950-3

a) Causes

On 25 June 1950 90,000 North Korean soldiers, battle-hardened by their experience in the Chinese civil war and spearheaded by 150 T-34 tanks, smashed through South Korea's border defences. They had been ordered across the 38th parallel by Kim Il Sung, the leader of North Korea. Kim was a nationalist who wanted to unify the Korean peninsula under communist rule. He was encouraged by the extent of support for communism in the south and growing opposition to the regime of Syngman Rhee. He believed that he would be welcomed by many South Koreans as a liberator and champion of Korean unification. Indeed recent historians of the conflict have seen the invasion as an episode in an on-going civil war in Korea between north and south. Kim thought that the war would last a matter of days. This estimate was based in part on Acheson's defence perimeter speech in January 1950, in which he had omitted South Korea from a list of countries which the United States would automatically defend in the event of aggression. Kim was in any case deeply hostile to the United States. Japan had occupied Korea between 1910 and 1945 and he resented the American policy of rebuilding Japan as a regional power. He had also fought with Mao against the Japanese in Manchuria and he was mindful of the attempt by the United States in the Chinese civil war to defeat his old ally by assisting Jiang's Nationalists.

As early as January 1950 Stalin had cautiously agreed to Kim's invasion plans, but in a meeting between the two leaders in April he warned Kim that Russia would not intervene directly in the conflict. Stalin told the North Korean leader, 'If you should get kicked in the teeth, I shall not lift a finger.' Stalin did, however, send military supplies and advisers to North Korea in May and June 1950. As ever, he was looking after the interests of the Soviet Union. He did not want Russia to become involved in another war so soon after the end of the Second World War. Yet if Kim could conquer South Korea with his assistance, it would be to the advantage of the Soviet Union. A united communist Korea would further secure Russia's borders, threaten America's new ally Japan, and place at his disposal South Korea's extensive reserves of lead (a commodity temporarily in short supply in the Soviet Union). The other major figure in the communist world, Mao, also gave limited support to Kim's invasion plans. Kim was an old ally but Mao had his own reasons for offering no firm promise of military assistance. The Chinese communists had only just won the civil war, and Mao's immediate priorities were establishing communist rule in China and defeating the remaining Nationalist forces on the island of Taiwan.

America's initial response to North Korea's invasion was to rush military supplies to Korea. Then on 27 June the United States sponsored a resolution in the United Nations Security Council calling for military action against North Korea. The resolution was passed only because the Soviet Union was boycotting meetings of the Security Council in response to the American refusal to accept newly communist China as a permanent member of the Council. Three days later Truman ordered American troops stationed in Japan into Korea. At the time the president enjoyed widespread support for his decisive action. Both houses of Congress cheered the announcement that US troops were being despatched to Korea, and opinion polls in July recorded that 75 per cent of the American public approved of Truman's decision. US soldiers formed part of a UN army which included South Korean forces and contingents from 15 other countries. Although outwardly a UN exercise, intervention in Korea was essentially an American operation. The United States committed 260,000 troops, while UN soldiers from other nations never exceeded 35,000. The South Korean army and the UN forces were also placed under the unified command of General Douglas MacArthur, who was accountable to Truman in Washington.

Only five years after the defeat of Germany and Japan America was again at war. As recently as January 1950 Acheson had implied that under the defensive perimeter strategy American forces would not be used in Korea. Why then in June 1950 did the United States commit itself to a land war in Asia? Policy-makers wrongly believed that Kim had been directed to invade by Moscow. They could not accept that Kim was acting independently. The crossing of the 38th parallel was interpreted as a clear instance of Soviet expansionism. If the United States did nothing in Korea, then neighbouring states would fall to

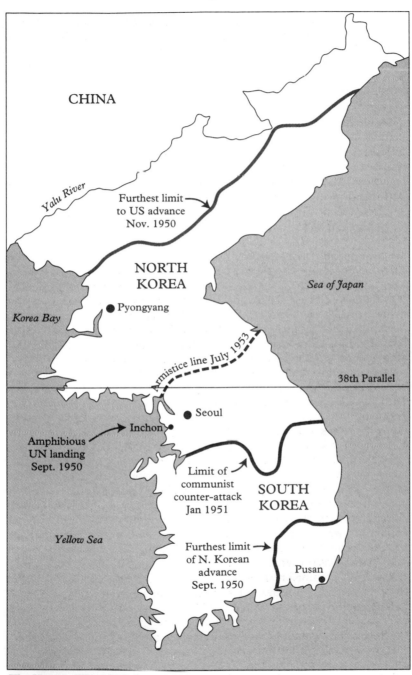

CHINA

Yalu River

Furthest limit
to US advance
Nov. 1950

NORTH
KOREA

Sea of Japan

● Pyongyang

Korea Bay

Armistice line July 1953

38th Parallel

● Seoul

Inchon ●

Amphibious
UN landing
Sept. 1950

Limit of
communist
counter-attack
Jan 1951

SOUTH
KOREA

Yellow Sea

Furthest limit
of N. Korean
advance
Sept. 1950

● Pusan

The Korean War 1950-3

Soviet communism (the domino theory). Truman used a variant of the domino theory to justify American intervention: 'If we let Korea down, the Soviet will keep right on going and swallow up one piece of Asia after another ... If we were to let Asia go, the Near East would collapse and no telling what would happen in Europe.' The President believed that a firm response would rapidly thwart Soviet expansion: '[Korea] is the Greece of the Far East. If we are tough enough now, if we stand up to them like we did in Greece three years ago, they won't take any next steps.' On another level, the invasion of South Korea provided a test of America's credibility and ability to resist communism across the world. American inaction in Korea might engender a mood of defeatism in the peoples of western Europe and Japan. They would lose confidence in the United States and see the Soviet Union as a more reliable ally.

b) Overview

The war opened badly for the Americans. In August the North Koreans captured Seoul, the capital of South Korea. The conditions for fighting were unpleasant. It was the monsoon season and temperatures exceeded 100 degrees. Thirsty American soldiers drank standing water from rice fields fertilised by human waste and were afflicted by dysentery. By September the UN forces occupied only a toehold around Pusan on the southern tip of the Korean peninsula. The most dramatic and fluid phase of the conflict now began. MacArthur mounted an outflanking movement and in a daring amphibious operation landed UN forces behind enemy lines at the port of Inchon and pushed on towards the 38th parallel. At the same time UN troops broke out of the Pusan perimeter and advanced rapidly north. Truman now made a fateful decision. He jettisoned the original war aim of simply expelling North Korean forces from South Korea and authorised the crossing of the 38th parallel. The North Korean capital, Pyongyang, fell while MacArthur raced towards the Yalu River, which separated North Korea from China. The United States was no longer pursuing a policy of containment but one of rollback, the recovery of territory under communist control. This action was prompted by a desire to teach communist aggressors a lesson, expectations of a quick victory and the prospect of a united Korea within the US orbit. The restoration of the 38th parallel as the border between South and North Korea would always leave South Korea open to attack from the north. Rollback would drive communism out of the Korean peninsula permanently and result in a morale-boosting victory in the Cold War. Importantly, the decision to cross the 38th parallel was based on intelligence reports that neither the Soviet Union nor China would intervene in the war.

Those intelligence reports were flawed. MacArthur knew that Chinese forces were massing beyond the Yalu River, but their numbers had been grossly underestimated at 30,000. MacArthur also misread the movement of Chinese armies as a bluff. The Chinese leader, Mao, had not wanted to intervene but now felt compelled to do so. The presence of American troops on the Chinese border was a threat to national security. Mao also feared that Jiang might launch a counter-revolution within China with the support of US armed forces. At first Mao sent a few 'volunteers' across the border and they helped to halt MacArthur's advance. They then deliberately withdrew into the mountains as a test of American intentions. When MacArthur continued his offensive, 260,000 Chinese troops poured across the Yalu River. The bleakest days of the Korean War followed for the United States. In temperatures 20 to 30 degrees below zero 40,000 US troops in north-east Korea were penned in by the Chinese and had to fight their way out before being evacuated from the port of Hungnam. In December the UN forces suffered 11,000 casualties in two days. On one of those two days 3,000 US soldiers had died. The communists now launched a major counter-offensive, reoccupying Pyongyang and recapturing Seoul in January 1951.

In Washington a flustered Truman briefly considered using atomic weapons against the Chinese to force their withdrawal from the war, but then rejected the option of all-out war with China, aware that it might lead to world war with the Soviet Union. Truman and Acheson took the crucial decision to abandon the objective of unifying Korea by military means and reverted to the original America war aim of restoring the 38th parallel as the border between North and South Korea. The United States had decided to fight a limited war in Korea. A limited war meant that the United States was confining the conflict to one place and pursuing a specific objective which was the independence of South Korea. Such a war minimised the risk of a confrontation with the Soviet Union. The strategy of limited war suited Stalin, who had never wanted war with the United States. As soon as the conflict had started, he had withdrawn Soviet military advisers from Korea and recalled ships headed for North Korea with military supplies. In 1950 he had broken his promise to Mao to provide air cover and military supplies for the advancing Chinese armies. Later he did give some help to the Chinese and North Korean forces but caution was the keynote of the Soviet approach. Stalin carefully avoided any action which might result in war with the United States. Russian pilots flying Mig-15s were under orders not to enter South Korean airspace, while Russian intelligence officers who interrogated UN prisoners of war wore Chinese uniforms.

In 1951 the priority for the United States on the battlefield was to drive the communist forces behind the 38th parallel. The war effort was hindered by disagreements between Truman and MacArthur. MacArthur was not happy about fighting a limited war and made his commitment to total victory public. In April Truman relieved him of his command on the grounds that the military must obey the orders of the civilian commander-in-chief, namely the president. MacArthur returned to the United States a hero. Truman's decision angered both American politicians and people. MacArthur was backed by the 'China lobby', a network of Republican (and a few Democrat) Congressmen who blamed Truman for the 'loss' of China, believed that the State Department was populated with communist sympathisers, and wanted not only total victory in Korea but the recovery of China. Public opinion was also frustrated by a limited war incurring high casualties and unable to deliver a quick victory over the communists. The conflict in Korea was dubbed 'Truman's war' and the President remained deeply unpopular for the remainder of his second term of office.

On 19 April MacArthur addressed both houses of Congress.

1 Our victory was complete when Red China intervened with numerically superior ground forces. I called for reinforcements, but was informed that reinforcements were not available. I made it clear that if not permitted to destroy the enemy forces north of the
5 Yalu, if not permitted to utilise the friendly Chinese forces of some 600,000 men on Formosa [Taiwan], if not permitted to blockade the China coast to prevent the Chinese Reds from getting succour from without ... the position of command from the military standpoint forbade victory ... In war there can be no substitute for
10 victory.

The following month both MacArthur and members of the Truman administration were asked to testify before the Senate Armed Services and Foreign Relations Committees, which were responsible for monitoring the president's defence and foreign policies. George Marshall, who had been recalled by Truman as Secretary of Defense, put the administration's side of the argument.

1 Now, as to the basic differences of judgement which exist between General MacArthur on the one hand ... the President on the other hand. Our objective in Korea continues to be the defeat of the aggression and the restoration of peace ... to confine the conflict in
5 Korea and to prevent it spreading into a Third World War. General MacArthur on the other hand would have us, on our own initiative, carry the conflict beyond Korea against the mainland of Communist China ... He would have us accept ... involvement not only in an extension of the war with Red China, but in all-out war
10 with the Soviet Union ... at the expense of losing our allies and wrecking the coalition of free peoples throughout the world.

MacArthur's successor was Lieutenant General Matthew Ridgway. Even before the former's dismissal the UN forces had begun to enjoy limited success on the ground. In February 1951 a powerful counter-attack, Operation Killer, had been launched. In March 1951

Operation Ripper followed. Superior firepower and command of the air enabled UN troops to recross the 38th parallel and for the rest of the war the battle front stabilised along a line 150 miles long just north of the parallel. During the next two years UN forces held their position while probing the enemy lines in a series of actions known as 'active defence'.

Stalemate on the ground encouraged both sides to seek a negotiated end to hostilities. Peace talks began in July 1951 but dragged on for two years. There were two main obstacles to agreement. One was Stalin. He was influencing negotiations from afar and urging Mao and Kim to extract further concessions from the United States in return for an end to the war. The second was the issue of the repatriation of prisoners of war. The North Koreans and the Chinese rejected the principle that prisoners of war should not be returned to their native countries against their will. The death of Stalin in March 1953 and compromise on the matter of repatriation eventually resulted in an armistice in July 1953. Under the terms of the ceasefire a line corresponding roughly to the 38th parallel was confirmed as the boundary between North and South Korea. Three years of fighting had changed nothing. Although it never escalated into a global confrontation with the Soviet Union, the Korean War was a conflict on a large scale. At one point a quarter of a million US troops were ranged against communist forces numbering 865,000. Korea had been the scene of a limited but costly war: the United States lost 33,629 dead from battle, South Korea 415,000, and the UN allies 3,000, while total communist dead and wounded were estimated at two million.

c) Consequences

The consequences of the Korean War were far-reaching. Engagement in Korea necessitated a substantial rise in US defence production. Output in 1953 was seven times greater than in 1950, but this massive increase in US defence capabilities occurred not only for the narrow purpose of fighting the war in Korea. Working on the false assumption that Stalin had directed Kim to invade South Korea, policy-makers reasoned that Soviet-inspired aggression in Korea might be followed by similar moves elsewhere in the world. The United States must therefore be ready to fight a series of limited wars against communism around the globe. If necessary, communism must be contained by military means.

This strategy presupposed a permanent expansion of America's armed forces and a constant state of military readiness. The United States must attempt to achieve near-parity in conventional forces with the Soviet Union and maintain nuclear superiority. Accordingly Truman now supported the increases in military spending proposed in NSC 68 which he had been unwilling to endorse prior to the Korean War. A member of the State Department commented, 'We were sweating over NSC 68 and then, thank God, Korea came along.' In

1950 Truman asked Congress for $10 billion to spend on America's armed forces, $260 million for the hydrogen bomb project and $4 billion in military aid for US allies. Korea marked the militarisation of the cold Cold War. Washington believed that the United States could only circumscribe Soviet power from a position of military strength, which meant enlarged conventional forces and continuing superiority in strategic weapons.

Since western Europe was regarded as the most likely area for Soviet expansion, NATO was immediately strengthened. The organisation was given an expanded secretariat and a unified command structure working to a US Supreme Commander, the first of whom was Dwight Eisenhower. Four US divisions were also despatched to Europe as reinforcements. In 1951 the membership of NATO was enlarged to include Greece and Turkey. Military bases in Turkey gave the United States the capability of launching air raids against the southern Soviet Union and were a useful platform for blocking any attempted Soviet advance on the oilfields of the Middle East. The United States also encouraged its NATO partners to increase their military spending in an attempt to make NATO an effective shield against Soviet aggression. Between 1951 and 1955 the US sent $25 billion in aid to its NATO allies, but such sums were contingent upon increases in their own defence budgets. Britain, for example, allocated 8.7 per cent of gross domestic product (GDP) to defence spending in 1951 in comparison with 5.9 per cent the previous year.

West German rearmament was also central to the reinforcement of NATO. As soon as war broke out in Korea, the United States wanted West Germany to share in the defence of western Europe. The Americans were not advocating an independent West German army, but West German membership of NATO. France was not so enthusiastic about the prospect of a rearmed West Germany, and attempted to delay the whole enterprise and impose as many limits on German rearmament as possible. In October 1950 the French put forward the Pleven Plan, under which West Germany would join not NATO but a European army called the European Defence Community (EDC). The size and number of West German units would be strictly limited. The United States agreed to EDC as a means of securing French support for the urgent priority of West German rearmament.

America's commitment to West German rearmament placed the West German Chancellor, Adenauer, in a powerful position. Claiming that very few Germans wished to rearm so soon after the horrors of the war, he traded West German consent to rearmament for a rapid recovery of German sovereignty. The price the United States paid for West German rearmament was the abolition of remaining occupation controls in 1952 and the recognition of West Germany as a full sovereign state. The political and economic reconstruction of West Germany had in any case been a long-term objective of the United

States and a vital aspect of the strategy of containment in Europe, but there is no doubt that the Korean War and the desire of the United States to rearm Germany accelerated the end of the occupation and West Germany's achievement of full statehood.

West Germany's transition from wartime enemy to post-war ally in the face of the Soviet threat was paralleled by Japan in the Far East. The Korean War hastened Japan's economic as well as political recovery. During the war Japan was home to hundreds of thousands of American soldiers, and their spending power provided a valuable stimulus to Japanese economic growth. The political reconstruction of Japan was confirmed in the San Francisco peace treaty (1951), which ended the state of war bewteen the United States and Japan, restored sovereignty to Japan and terminated the occupation with effect from 1952. In return for independence America secured Japan's signature to a Mutual Security Agreement negotiated at the same time as the peace treaty, which guaranteed the United States military bases both in Japan and on the island of Okinawa. The Japanese islands therefore formed a major bulwark against further communist expansion in the Far East. The Yoshida Letter provided further evidence of Japan's central importance to the strategy of confining communist influence in Asia. Under this agreement the Japanese Prime Minister Shigeru Yoshida had to agree to a trade embargo with communist China. The United States hoped that economic isolation would weaken and ultimately bring down Mao's regime. Washington also feared that a burgeoning trade relationship between Japan and China would be followed by closer political ties and the detachment of Japan from the US sphere of influence. In the Yoshida Letter Japan also promised to trade with Taiwan.

US policy towards Taiwan had changed as soon as the Korean War started. After the defeat of the Nationalists America had finally given up on Jiang Jieshi and had no formal plans to help him resist an invasion by Mao Zedong's forces. But in June 1950 Truman immediately ordered the Seventh Fleet to the Taiwan Straits to defend the island against possible communist invasion. The Korean War scuppered any remaining chance that the United States might recognise the People's Republic and build Mao up as an Asian Tito, capable of standing up to Moscow in the same way as the Yugoslavian communist leader, who had broken with Stalin in 1948. Indeed the United States recognised Taiwan as the only official Chinese state until 1971, when recognition was accorded to mainland China. Jiang was the recipient of substantial economic and military aid, and the denial of the island of Taiwan to China was an important means of limiting the power of Chinese communism in Asia.

Japan's re-emergence as a sovereign state alarmed its recent wartime enemies in the Pacific. Countries like Australia and New Zealand saw the new Japan as both an economic rival and a potential aggressor. Just as American policy-makers had had to secure French compliance with the reconstruction of west Germany, so they had to align Australia and New Zealand behind the policy of promoting Japan. Accordingly the United States signed the ANZUS Pact. Under the terms of this security agreement all parties agreed to help each other in the event of aggression against Australasia. The ANZUS Pact was mutually beneficial. The United States would protect Australia and New Zealand against a resurgent Japan, while Australia and New Zealand would help the United States defend the Pacific against communist incursions.

The Korean War also impacted on US policy towards south-east Asia. Indochina was seen as the key to the region. In an attempt to eliminate communism in Vietnam the United States threw its weight behind the French in their war with the Vietminh. The American view of Ho Chi Minh as an agent of the Kremlin was only confirmed by events in Korea. By the early 1950s the United States was spending $1 billion a year in military assistance to the French. The fate of south-east Asia and the future of Japan were interdependent. China no longer existed as a marketplace for Japanese goods and a source of raw materials, so Indochina had to fill the vacuum and serve as Japan's economic hinterland. Japan and the non-communist countries of south-east Asia must be integrated into a regional economy guaranteeing mutual prosperity.

There is no doubt that the Korean War was a pivotal event in the Cold War. It marked an acceleration but not a reorientation of American policy. Measures such as the reinforcement of NATO, West German sovereignty and potential rearmament, a Japanese peace treaty, increased economic aid to anti-communist regimes in south-east Asia and a Pacific security pact had all been under active consideration before hostilities in Korea, but all these occurred sooner than they otherwise would have done as a result of the Korean War. War in Korea also accelerated the globalisation of the Cold War. After Korea the United States had new military commitments across the world. American soldiers defended points as far afield as the frontier of western Europe and the 38th parallel in Korea. These new commitments were reflected in permanently higher levels of defence spending. In 1950 defence spending stood at $13.1 billion. Under the impact of Korea it reached a high of $50.4 billion and was never less than $40 billion a year for the remainder of the 1950s. War in Korea also brought about a militarisation of American policy. Before Korea the avoidance of committing US troops to a war on the Asian land-mass had been an axiom of American diplomacy; after Korea the United States was ready to deploy troops anywhere in order to defend the 'free world'.

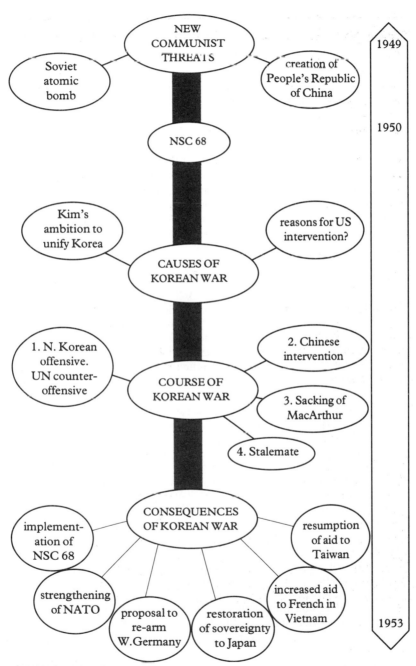

Summary - Escalation: Global Cold War, Hot War in Korea, 1949-53

Making Notes on '*Escalation: Global Cold War, Hot War in Korea, 1949-53*'

As before, use the end-of-chapter summary and the chapter headings to provide the structure for your notes. Once again, it might be helpful to organise your notes around answers to a set of questions. What were the aims of the US policy of containment in 1949? What was the impact of the Soviet atomic test and the communist victory in the Chinese civil war on US policy? What were the main proposals of NSC 68? How did those proposals differ from previous US policy? Why did the US intervene militarily to defend South Korea in 1950? You may wish to make only brief notes on the actual course of the Korean War as you are unlikely ever to be required to write a narrative account of the war. What were the consequences of the Korean War for US policy? Use the end-of-chapter summary diagram to identify the main points here.

Answering essay questions on '*Escalation: Global Cold War, Hot War in Korea, 1949-53*'

The following are some typical essay questions on this phase of the Cold War.

1   Examine the effects of (a) the end of the atomic monopoly, and (b) the 'fall' of China on US policy 1949-50.
2   Why did the United States extend only limited economic aid to the Chinese Nationalists under Jiang Jieshi, yet intervene militarily in the defence of South Korea?
3   To what extent did the Korean War prove to be a turning point in US policy in the Cold War?

The key word in question 1 is 'effects'. The question is testing your ability to identify and explain the consequences or results of the two events mentioned in the question. Deal with each event in turn and try to identify actions which the United States took in response to each event. You might discuss the fear generated in Washington as a result of the Soviet atomic test, the impact of the test on America's own nuclear weapons programme and the link between the end of the US atomic monopoly and the review of national security policy embodied in NSC 68. In the case of the 'fall' of China you might explain how the US briefly attempted a 'wedge' strategy, the failure of such a strategy and the impact of the establishment of the People's Republic of China on the American perception of the worldwide communist threat.

Questions 2 is a 'why' question and asks you to give reasons for two contrasting policy decisions. You will need to have read the appropriate sections of Chapter 3 in order to deal with the first part of the question.

You must try to address the apparent contradiction posed by the question. Both Jiang in China and Syngman Rhee in South Korea were resisting a communist threat on the Asian land-mass. In the first instance the US offered Jiang only limited economic assistance; in the second instance the US committed itself to a land war. You should try to explain why the US extended only limited aid to Jiang in terms of the priorities of US policy, the principle of avoiding a land war in Asia, the defensive perimeter strategy and the personality of Jiang. How else might you explain US policy towards Jiang? The decision to intervene militarily in Korea was a departure from previous policy and it is up to you to analyse why US policy-makers believed that the circumstances in Korea warranted a turn in policy.

Question 3 falls into the now familiar 'to what extent' category. 'Turning point' is also a key term in the question. If you are arguing that the Korean War was a turning point, then you have to highlight major changes in US policy which occurred directly as a result of the Korean War. If you are arguing the other way, you will be looking for the continuity of US policy before and after the Korean War, or perhaps you will be arguing that the changes in US policy would have happened with or without Korea - that the Korean War merely meant that those changes happened sooner. Which line of argument you adopt will depend on the opinions you have formed from reading the chapter. This is a case where the examiner will give equal credit whichever interpretation you present. The important factors will be the coherence of your argument, and the way in which you support it with appropriate evidence. Remember that selective quotation from primary sources is a useful method of both enlivening your essay and supporting a particular point in your argument.

Source-based questions on 'Escalation: Global Cold War, Hot War in Korea, 1949-53'

MacArthur and the Korean War
Read the two extracts on page 70 and answer the following questions.
a) In the context of the extracts explain the following: i) 'Red China' (line 1); (1 mark) ii) 'coalition of free peoples' (line 11) (1 mark)
b) Both extracts are from evidence before Congressional committees. Why might a historian be cautious about accepting the reliability of such evidence? (5 marks)
c) To what extent do the two extracts agree on both the aims and the means the United States should adopt in the Korean War? (8 marks)

CHAPTER 5

Co-existence and Confrontation: Eisenhower's Cold War, 1953-61

1 Introduction

When Dwight D. Eisenhower defeated the Democrat Adlai Stevenson in the 1952 presidential election, he became the first Republican to occupy the White House for twenty years. In many respects he appeared to have the ideal qualifications for overseeing America foreign policy at the height of the Cold War. Eisenhower, nicknamed 'Ike', was a career soldier with a distinguished military background. He had commanded the Allied armies invading Normandy in 1944, and after the war had served as US Army Chief of Staff and as the first Supreme Commander of NATO.

For most of his presidency Eisenhower and his Secretary of State, John Foster Dulles, jointly steered US foreign policy. The common perception of Eisenhower was of a relaxed, hands-off president content to leave the details of policy-making to subordinates and more interested in improving his golf swing than in leading America. The reality was rather different. The relationship between Eisenhower and Dulles was in fact a close partnership. Ike formulated the objectives of policy and was never as out of touch with the day-to-day business of government as his critics suggested. Ike and Dulles were bound together by a fierce anti-communism. Dulles was a public and vociferous opponent of the Soviet system. Eisenhower's sentiments were more private but just as strongly held.

Ike's period in office has often been seen as a time of relative stability in the Cold War. While it is true that the United States and the Soviet Union had learnt to co-exist with each other, there were also moments of high danger under Eisenhower. America threatened the use of nuclear weapons against the People's Republic of China at least three times. Indeed relations between America and China remained very tense throughout Eisenhower's presidency. There were brief thaws in US-Soviet relations in 1955 and 1959, overtaken on the first occasion by the Hungarian uprising and the Suez crisis and on the second by the shooting down of a U-2 spy plane over Soviet territory. However, Sino- and Soviet-American relations under Eisenhower were as frequently in crisis as in equilibrium.

2 Containment under Eisenhower: The New Look

Eisenhower's arrival in office prompted a re-examination of how the United States should respond to international communism. By the end of 1953 a new strategy of containment had emerged, entitled the 'New

Look'. In fact the New Look was not as novel as its name implied. The objectives of containment remained fixed. The fundamental purpose of containment was still negative, to prevent the extension of Soviet communism outside those areas where it was already established. As a Marxist-Leninist state, the Soviet Union, according to the Americans, displayed an innate expansionist impulse. However, it was believed that, denied opportunities to expand, the Soviet system would self-destruct and the Soviet empire in eastern Europe would crumble. This was the classic theory of containment as expounded by George Kennan in 1946.

Moreover, the methods of containment employed by the Eisenhower administration were in many respects similar to those used under Truman. The United States continued to build a global web of anti-communist alliances designed to encircle the Soviet Union and check the spread of communism. American military power also remained an important tool of containment. American servicemen were stationed around the globe, either in place to defend vulnerable areas like West Berlin and South Korea against communist encroachment or to be despatched quickly to a scene of communist aggression from one of America's vast network of overseas bases. Huge sums in aid continued to be sent to forces resisting communist insurgency, such as Ngo Dinh Diem's government in South Vietnam after 1954.

Even one of the potential differences between Truman's and Eisenhower's national security policies turned out to be more of a similarity than a difference. In the presidential election campaign of 1952 Dulles criticised the passive posture of the Truman administration and promised 'rollback' and the liberation of eastern European countries under Soviet dominion. At one point Eisenhower had to rein in the aggressive Dulles. He endorsed the objective of liberation but emphasised that it must occur by peaceful means only. Yet, in the event, the pledge of liberation proved to be only campaign rhetoric. Under Ike America acknowledged the integrity of the Soviet sphere of influence and no attempt was made to recover by force territory already in the hands of the communists. After the armistice of 1953 the sovereignty of North Korea was respected by the United States and the status quo in Europe remained intact. Rebellions in East Germany in 1953 and Poland and Hungary in 1956 were tacitly encouraged by the Americans but not exploited as an opportunity to challenge the Soviet Union and force the withdrawal of those states from the eastern bloc.

Nevertheless, there were significant differences between Truman's and Eisenhower's strategies of containment. The most important of these was an increased reliance on nuclear weapons under Ike. Indeed, this was at the heart of the New Look. In the event of war with the Soviet Union nuclear weapons were now to be regarded as a weapon of first and not of last resort. A National Security document in 1953 stated, 'The US will consider nuclear weapons to be available for use as other munitions.' Ike put it in simpler terms to a group of Congressional leaders in 1954. Nuclear weapons would allow the United States 'to blow the hell out of them in a hurry if they start anything'. Dulles labelled this approach the doctrine of massive retaliation. He had a clear-sighted view of how the US nuclear arsenal could not only deter communist aggression but also further the goals of US diplomacy. America could threaten the use of nuclear weapons in order to extract concessions from communist adversaries. Yet the fact that the Soviet Union now possessed nuclear weapons of its own made nuclear blackmail a dangerous tactic. Dulles vividly articulated the diplomacy of brinkmanship in an interview with *Life* magazine in 1956: 'The ability to get to the verge without getting into the war is the necessary art ... If you try to run away from it, if you are scared to go to the brink, you are lost.'

The central place of nuclear weapons in the New Look presupposed a

"Don't Be Afraid—I Can Always Pull You Back"

Don't be Afraid - I can always pull you back

smaller role for conventional forces. Eisenhower was determined to cut the number of personnel in the American armed services. In this sense the New Look rejected the conclusions of NSC 68, which had envisaged a build-up of both conventional and nuclear forces. Ike believed that the United States could not afford to do both. As a soldier he had a keen appreciation of the relationship between the means and ends of a conflict. He was committed to victory in the Cold War, but at a price America could afford. The Cold War must be waged within available means. The rationale of the New Look was to curb the costs of containing Soviet communism. Ike chose the expansion of America's nuclear arsenal over the continued increase in conventional forces as the cheaper and more effective method of combating communism. It was a high technology/low manpower strategy which in a popular phrase of the day represented 'more bang for the buck'.

In two other important respects Eisenhower's policy of containment diverged from Truman's. Truman had used covert operations selectively, but Ike was far more willing to sanction such actions. He was familiar with intelligence operations from his time as a soldier and often referred to the importance of intelligence as a basis for decision-making. The fact that the Director of the CIA, Allen Dulles, was the brother of the Secretary of State also made for a closer relationship between the CIA and the executive than had existed under Truman. Indeed Eisenhower's presidency has been seen as a milestone in the history of the CIA. Both the scale and the frequency of CIA operations grew under Ike and he regarded undercover action as a routine instrument of foreign policy. Covert actions also had the advantage of being quick, cheap and beyond the scrutiny of Congress.

Eisenhower also regarded negotiation both with the Soviet Union and with the People's Republic of China as a legitimate part of the policy of containment. Within Eisenhower a gut hostility to communism vied with an instinct to act as a peacemaker and improve US-Soviet relations. Ike was a great believer in personal diplomacy and was gloomy about the future course of the Cold War unless personal initiatives were taken by leaders to reduce tension. In 1953 he confided in his aide Emmet Hughes: 'We are in an armaments race. Where will it lead us? At worst, to atomic warfare. At best, to robbing every people and nation on earth of the fruits of their own toil.' There was a full US-Soviet summit under Ike in 1955, a further meeting between Ike and Khrushchev in 1959 and one abortive summit in 1960. In 1954 Secretary of State Dulles met the Chinese Foreign Minister Zhou Enlai (Chou En-lai) to discuss the situation in Vietnam. Negotiations at ambassadorial level between China and the United States continued intermittently for the remainder of Eisenhower's presidency. For much of Truman's presidency diplomacy of this kind would have been unthinkable. Under Truman the last meeting even at foreign minister level between the superpowers had occurred in 1948.

3 Containment in Practice: The Global Cold War under Eisenhower

a) Europe

Europe formed a relatively stable theatre in the Cold War during Eisenhower's administration. Rebellions against communist rule in eastern Europe provided opportunities for American intervention in the region and the loosening of the Soviet bloc. On the other side, Soviet proposals for a nuclear-free central Europe and renewed pressure on the Western powers in Berlin in 1958 threatened to alter the balance of power in Europe. Ultimately, however, the status quo continued and the frontier between the American sphere of influence and the Eastern bloc remained unchanged.

The first signs of protest against Soviet rule occurred in East Germany shortly after Stalin's death in June 1953. Workers mounted anti-Soviet demonstrations in the streets of East Berlin and went on general strike. They also demanded better living standards and free elections. The insurrection was put down by Soviet troops and in East Berlin Russian tanks drove protesters off the streets. This was the first test of the promise made by Dulles during his Senate confirmation hearings to bring about 'the liberation of these captive peoples'. In the event the only action taken by the United States was to broadcast the demands of the East German protesters across Germany on the airwaves of the American-sponsored Radio Free Europe.

Events in Hungary in 1956 also exposed the emptiness of Dulles's promise. In October 1956 the reformer Imre Nagy was installed as premier and immediately called for the evacuation of Soviet troops from Hungary and the withdrawal of Hungary from the Warsaw Pact. Free elections were also part of the reformers' manifesto. Briefly it appeared as if this revolution had been successful, yet on 4 November 200,000 Soviet troops and 4,000 tanks entered Budapest, according to the Russians, 'to help the Hungarian people crush the black forces of reaction and counter-revolution'. On that day an estimated 50,000 Hungarians lost their lives. Nagy was replaced by the pro-Soviet Janos Kadar as leader.

Again the Americans did no more than broadcast anti-Soviet propaganda and the demands of the rebels on Radio Free Europe. In the first volume of his presidential memoirs published in 1963, *Mandate for Change*, Eisenhower explained the American position.

1 The Hungarian uprising, from its beginning to its bloody suppression, was an occurrence that inspired in our nation feelings of sympathy and admiration for the rebels, anger and disgust for their Soviet oppressors ... An expedition ... across neutral Austria,

5 Titoist Yugoslavia or Communist Czechoslovakia, was out of the
question. The fact was that Hungary could not be reached by any
United Nations or United States units without traversing such
territory. Unless the major nations of Europe would, without
10 delay, ally themselves spontaneously with us, we could do nothing.
Sending United States troops alone into Hungary through hostile
or neutral territory would have involved us in general war. And too,
if the United Nations overriding a certain Soviet veto, decided that
the military and other resources of member nations should be used
15 to drive the Soviets from Hungary, we would inevitably have a
major conflict.

For their part the Russians made two attempts to change the situation in
Europe in their favour. The first was the Rapacki Plan (1958), named
after Poland's Foreign Minister. The Plan proposed a phased reduction
in conventional forces and a nuclear-free zone in central Europe
encompassing East and West Germany, Poland and Czechoslovakia.
The United States promptly rejected the Plan. The removal of nuclear
weapons from West Germany was at odds with the nuclear-based theory
of deterrence enshrined in the New Look. Also a nuclear-free West
Germany would be without its safety net. It would be exposed to
invasion from the east by numerically superior Warsaw Pact ground
forces. At the end of 1958 Khrushchev demanded that the Western
powers quit Berlin within six months. The United States refused to do
so for much the same reasons it had done in 1948. Ike warned that a
Soviet takeover of West Berlin ran the risk of massive retaliation, but
said that he would be happy to discuss the whole issue of Berlin in return
for the Soviets lifting their ultimatum. This the Soviet Union did and
Berlin was one of the matters discussed at the 1959 meeting between Ike
and Khrushchev. The latest Berlin crisis had been temporarily defused.

The United States encountered difficulties in Europe not only with
the Soviet Union but with its own partners in the Western alliance,
principally France. In 1954 the French changed their position on West
German rearmament. Previously France had agreed to accept West
German rearmament inside a European Defence Community (EDC), a
European army with a separate identity from NATO. Now, however,
the French government rejected the EDC treaty and called for further
safeguards to be imposed on West German rearmament. The
importance the United States attached to rearming West Germany was
illustrated by Dulles's response to the French. He spoke of 'an agonising
reappraisal' of America's military commitments in western Europe. The
threat was clear: the United States might withdraw its troops from
western Europe and leave the region vulnerable to Soviet land armies.
Moreover, the western part of the continent might no longer enjoy the
protection offered by US nuclear weapons. This was a real threat in
1954, since no west European state had a nuclear deterrent of its own.

Eventually a solution was brokered by the British Prime Minister, Anthony Eden. West Germany would be admitted to NATO subject to certain severe restrictions designed to mollify the French: Britain would maintain four divisions and a tactical air force on the continent as a security guarantee to the French; Germany would not be allowed to manufacture chemical, biological or nuclear weapons; the German armed forces must not exceed 500,000 and would be under the command of the NATO Supreme Allied Commander in Europe. In May 1955 West Germany joined NATO, an act that was accepted not only by France but by the Soviet Union. The Russians recognised the West German state during a visit by Chancellor Adenauer to Moscow in 1955. The Soviet Union had finally reconciled itself to the fact that West Germany would be neither neutral nor part of a single German state within the Soviet bloc. Just as the Americans were forced to accept the integrity of the Eastern bloc, so the Russians had to acquiesce in the sovereignty of the states belonging to the Western alliance.

b) Asia

i) Korea

Under Eisenhower Asia was an altogether more volatile arena in the Cold War than Europe. The first outstanding issue confronting Ike's administration was the resolution of the Korean conflict. During his presidential campaign Ike had announced that he would himself go to Korea, and once in office he was personally committed to a speedy end to the war. Negotiations for an armistice foundered on the issue of repatriation of North Korean and Chinese prisoners who did not want to return to their native countries. Having agreed to send such prisoners to neutral countries which would decide their fate, the United States and China could not agree on which neutral countries. Ike applied pressure to the Chinese by hinting that the US might use atomic weapons against the Chinese mainland. In July 1953 the two sides agreed an end to hostilities. Ike warned the Chinese that any breach of the terms of the armistice might also bring a nuclear reprisal from the United States. Yet the American resort to nuclear blackmail was not the principal reason for the armistice. Both America and the People's Republic of China were keen to extricate themselves from an expensive and bloody war, and the death of Stalin in March 1953 removed an obstacle to the end of hostilities. The party least content with the armistice was Syngman Rhee, whose hopes of a united Korea under his leadership had now been extinguished.

ii) China, Taiwan and the Offshore Islands

Two small island groups lying in the Taiwan Straits between Taiwan and mainland China, the Quemoy and Matsu islands, were the cause of two major crises in Sino-American relations under Eisenhower. Both Quemoy and Matsu were garrisoned by Nationalist forces and seen by Jiang Jieshi as a platform for a military invasion of the mainland. In 1954 Jiang announced a 'holy war' against Chinese communism and promised an imminent attack. China in return threatened to invade Taiwan. In 1954 a foray against Quemoy and Matsu by Chinese communists was followed by a sustained bombardment of the islands. At the beginning of 1955 the Chinese communists also attacked the Tachen islands, another group of Nationalist-held islands near to Taiwan.

Hitherto relations between Jiang and Washington had been strained. Both Ike and Dulles suspected that Jiang wanted to use US soldiers to invade the Chinese mainland, which would have triggered a full-scale war with the Soviet Union. Nevertheless, the United States now fully supported Jiang and renewed its commitment to defend Taiwan. The shelling of the Quemoy and Matsu islands led to a mutual defence pact. The Americans promised to defend Taiwan against communist invasion. But in a simultaneous secret agreement Jiang had to accept that any invasion of the mainland must be subject to US approval. Washington had clipped Jiang's wings and lessened the likelihood of a major conflict involving the United States, China and the Soviet Union. The Chinese seizure of the Tachen Islands had two immediate consequences. Firstly Congress passed the Formosa Resolution allowing Eisenhower to take whatever military action he thought was necessary to defend Taiwan, and secondly Eisenhower announced that any move by the Chinese communists against Taiwan would be met by the use of nuclear weapons against a military target on mainland China. At this point the Chinese back-pedalled. The Chinese Premier Zhou Enlai said that China would only free Taiwan by peaceful means, and an informal cease-fire operated in the Taiwan Straits.

In 1958 the renewed bombardment of Quemoy and Matsu brought China and the United States to the brink of war. Dulles stated that Washington viewed these actions as the first stage of an attack on Taiwan. The Seventh Fleet was ordered into the Taiwan Straits, US forces in the Far East were put onto a war footing and a veiled threat of a nuclear strike against China was again issued. At the same time the Americans offered the Chinese the chance to negotiate, which they accepted. The outcome was a cease-fire in the Taiwan Straits. Dulles now entered into negotiations with Jiang. While he underlined the American pledge to defend Taiwan, he informed Jiang that the United States could in no way support an invasion of the mainland. He also persuaded Jiang to reduce the Nationalist military presence on the Quemoy and Matsu islands.

It is worth asking why America was prepared to risk war with China and the Soviet Union in order to defend the Quemoy and Matsu islands. Under Eisenhower, as under Truman, any instance of communist aggression was regarded as a test case of America's determination to defend the 'free world'. If the United States did nothing, it would send the wrong signals to anti-communist forces everywhere. Eisenhower firmly believed that to allow the communist Chinese to overrun the offshore islands would lead to a collapse of morale in Taiwan and its surrender to the People's Republic. An important outpost on the anti-communist perimeter in Asia would then disappear. American public and Congressional opinion also demanded a tough posture towards China. The 'China Lobby' was still active and campaigned for the recovery of mainland China. Neither Ike nor Dulles were opposed as a matter of principle to negotiations with the Chinese, but the state of American opinion simply did not allow an accommodation with the regime in Beijing. The United States was still tied to a 'Two Chinas' policy, which meant denying diplomatic recognition to the People's Republic and ensuring that China's place both in the United Nations General Assembly and on the UN Security Council was occupied not by the People's Republic but by Taiwan. The 'Two Chinas' policy would continue until 1971.

There is also convincing evidence that Dulles was aware that a firm American stance on the issue of the offshore islands might create cracks in the Sino-Soviet alliance. American pressure on the Chinese would confront the Soviet Union with an awkward choice about whether or not to support its communist ally in Asia. He noted in 1954 that Moscow's failure to support the Chinese over the offshore islands would 'put a serious strain on Soviet-ChiCom relations'. In talks with the Taiwanese Foreign Minister he observed, 'The whole communist domain is overextended ... The communist regimes are bound to crack. The leaders will fall out among themselves.' Other matters contributed to the growing rift between Beijing and Moscow, such as ideological differences and the legacy of mistrust created by Stalin's breach of his promise to provide Soviet air cover for Chinese troops in North Korea in 1950. But Mao was disappointed that the Russians were not more supportive on the question of the offshore islands. For his part Khrushchev wanted any confrontation with the United States to occur on Russian terms and at a time and place of the Soviet Union's choosing. He did not want to challenge the United States on the issue of the future of two tiny island chains in the Taiwan Straits.

iii) Indochina

American policy-makers continued to invest Indochina (Vietnam, Laos and Cambodia) with great strategic importance. Indochina held the key to south-east Asia. Eisenhower employed the well-worn domino theory to justify American intervention in the region. If Indochina fell to the communists, Thailand, Burma and Indonesia might follow. Indochina guarded the entrance to the rice-bowl of south-east Asia, which as a whole was vital to American interests. It was an important location for US military bases, a supplier of raw materials and a marketplace for Japanese goods.

The view that Ho Chi Minh was a Moscow-trained communist had led the Americans to sink $4 billion in aid into France's war against the Vietminh. The war had reached a critical phase by 1954. The French had chosen Dien Bien Phu in northern Vietnam as the site for a major battle with the Vietminh. The French forces were positioned in a valley while the Vietminh under the command of General Giap occupied the surrounding mountains. At this point the United States considered military intervention. The use of nuclear weapons against the Vietminh was discussed but Eisenhower dismissed it as an ineffective option in the circumstances. The deployment of American troops was also considered, but Ike attached two important conditions to such action. One was Congressional approval, the other was British participation. The message from Congress was 'no more Koreas', while Britain showed no interest in military action. Eisenhower therefore rejected the option of US military intervention. Meanwhile, starved of air supplies and subjected to heavy artillery bombardment, the French surrendered. Their defeat at Dien Bien Phu in 1954 marked the end of the French empire in Indochina.

The French and the Vietminh now opened negotiations in the presence of America and China and concluded the Geneva Accords in 1954. These agreements formally ended hostilities between France and Ho Chi Minh's forces, temporarily divided Vietnam along the 17th parallel and made provisions for national elections to unify the country within two years. Importantly, the United States did not sign the Geneva Accords, but promised not to break the agreements by the use of force. America's response to the Geneva Accords was to bolster South Vietnam as a stable non-communist state capable of resisting communist incursion from the north. The Americans wanted South Vietnam to develop along the lines of a second South Korea. A South-East Asia Treaty Organisation (SEATO) was established. Its members were the US, France, Britain, Australia, New Zealand, the Philippines, Thailand and Pakistan. It was modelled on NATO and its purpose was to prevent communist interference in South Vietnam, Laos and Cambodia. In reality, though. it was a pale imitation of NATO. Two of the region's major powers, India and Indonesia, refused to join. The circumstances under which SEATO members would use military force against an aggressor in the region were also unclear.

Within South Vietnam the United States removed the French-backed Bao Dai and installed their own candidate Ngo Dinh Diem as president. Some Americans doubted Diem's credentials as a figurehead for non-communist nationalism. He had collaborated with the Japanese during the war and was a Roman Catholic in a country where 90 per cent of the population were Buddhists. The Americans also opened a military mission in South Vietnam in 1954 designed to advise the South Vietnamese on methods of resisting communist infiltration from the north. Thus began America's long military commitment to the defence of South Vietnam. Two years later Eisenhower decided that South Vietnam would not participate in the nationwide elections agreed at Geneva on the grounds that Ho would have won such elections and overseen the creation of a united communist Vietnam. It has been estimated that Ho would have gained about 80 per cent of the vote in 1956.

Yet the decision not to hold elections did not secure South Vietnam against communism. To the north Ho Chi Minh consolidated his regime, while in the south in the late 1950s small bands of communists (Vietcong) formed themselves into military units and began to conduct guerrilla warfare against Diem's government. In 1960 they established a political arm, the National Liberation Front (NLF). They were supported by segments of the local population and by North Vietnam, which in 1959 had publicly affirmed its commitment to unite Vietnam by whatever means possible. Guerrilla warfare in the south was part of Ho's longer-term project to reunify the country.

The situation in adjacent Laos was also a source of concern in Washington. The pro-Western government of Laos created with the assistance of the CIA in 1959 was encountering opposition from the Pathet Lao, an indigenous communist group. There was evidence that Laos was being used as a conduit for supplies from North Vietnam to communist guerrillas in the south. By 1961 policy-makers in Washington were more worried about the fate of Laos than about that of Vietnam. Eisenhower's successors would discover that communism in Indochina was a problem that would not go away.

c) The Third World

The global character of the Cold War in the 1950s was underlined by its intrusion into new areas of the world. The Third World became an important new theatre in the conflict between the United States and the Soviet Union. The dissolution of the old European empires created a host of new nation states and potential allies for the two superpowers. Each competed with the other to recruit these new states into their alliance systems. Post-Stalinist Soviet diplomacy was more flexible and innovative and Russian leaders enticed emerging nations with offers of substantial economic and military aid. Decolonisation represented both an opportunity and a threat to the United States. America proved generally successful in drawing newly independent nation states into its orbit, but communism proved better placed to ride the tide of nationalism across those parts of the Third World which were still under colonial rule.

i) The Middle East

The broad outlines of American policy in the Middle East were to remain on friendly terms with the Arab states, minimise Soviet influence and maintain oil supples to the West. At one level the United States had always seen the Cold War as a battle for control of vital raw material resources, and thus the containment of communist power in an oil-rich region such as the Middle East was a key policy objective. Yet the projection of American influence in the Middle East was not an easy matter. Anti-American feelings ran deep in the region for two principal reasons. The post war Middle East was in the grip of nationalism and America was seen as an ally of the old colonial powers in the region, Britain and France. In addition the fact that the United States had sponsored the creation of the Jewish state of Israel in 1948 provoked Arab hostility. No Arab state had yet recognised Israel.

The first attempt to contain communism in the Middle East occurred in Iran in 1953. The instrument of containment was the CIA in what was the first major undercover operation of Eisenhower's presidency. In 1951 the Shah of Iran in response to public pressure had appointed the nationalist Mohammad Mossadeq as prime minister. One of Mossadeq's first actions was to regain control of a national economic resource by nationalising the Anglo-Iranian Oil Company which was half-owned by Britain. Britain and the United States then led a boycott of Iranian oil on the world market. The Americans were worried about Mossadeq's links with the Iranian communist party, the Tudeh. The British Foreign Secretary, Anthony Eden, reported that Eisenhower was obsessed by the fear of a communist Iran. In fact Mossadeq was not a communist, but the economic problems triggered by falling revenues from oil sales had dented his popularity and forced him into a closer partnership with the Tudeh in the Iranian parliament (Majlis).

In July 1953 Mossadeq appealed to the United States for aid, but the Americans had already decided to overthrow him in a plan codenamed Operation Ajax. The royalist General Zahedi was waiting in the wings to replace him. Washington now secured the Shah's support for the removal of Mossadeq, but initially the plan backfired. Mossadeq ignored the Shah's decree dismissing him from office and a political crisis ensued. The Shah fled his country in panic, Mossadeq dissolved the Majlis and turned to Moscow for help. CIA agents now exploited the situation by orchestrating fake communist demonstrations on the streets of the Iranian capital, Tehran, aimed at arousing fears of a communist takeover. They then mounted massive counter-demonstrations in favour of the Shah. American money was paid to street mobs who marched into the centre of Tehran and seized key government buildings. Nine hours of fighting followed in which soldiers loyal to Mossadeq were overcome. Mossadeq himself quit office, General Zahedi became the new Prime Minister and the Shah returned to Iran. Mossadeq had been

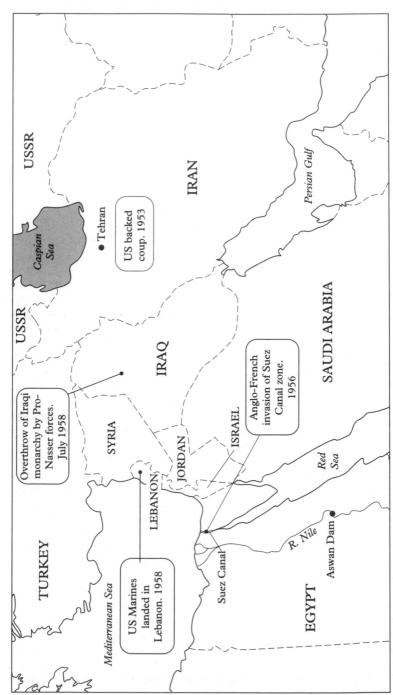

The Cold War in the Middle East under Eisenhower

unpopular with sections of the Iranian public, but there is no doubt that intervention by the CIA was partly responsible for his downfall. The CIA had participated in what amounted to a coup.

In the short term the results were favourable to the United States. Firstly, US oil companies acquired a stake in the distribution of Iranian oil. Secondly, Iran was now clearly aligned with the United States. Iran was a country of great geopolitical importance: it shared an extensive border with the Soviet Union and provided a northern entrance to the oilfields of the Middle East. Both the Shah of Iran and the new Prime Minister were now firmly pro-American. The alliance was subsequently primed by large amounts of American economic and military aid.

The Baghdad Pact was a further measure designed to exclude Soviet influence from the Middle East. It was formed in 1955 and its original members were Britain and Iraq, joined later by Iran and Pakistan. After 1959 it was known as the Central Treaty Organisation (CENTO). For the British the Pact was a means of maintaining their influence in the Middle East and their military bases in Iraq. The United States supported but did not join the Pact, occupying only observer status. The Americans feared that membership of the Pact might antagonise other Arab states, such as Egypt, and push those states closer to Moscow. Nevertheless, the Americans saw the Pact as the Middle Eastern link in the chain of anti-communist alliances which emerged in the 1940s and 1950s. A collection of friendly states on the southern flank of the Soviet Union grouped together in a security pact under British and American auspices was part of the global strategy of containment.

Egypt was the scene of the greatest Cold War crisis in the Middle East under Eisenhower. The Egyptian leader was President Nasser. He was a reformer, a moderniser and above all a nationalist. His ultimate ambition was a pan-Arab coalition of states under the leadership of Egypt. The construction of the Aswan Dam on the River Nile was part of his programme of economic modernisaton. The project would generate hydro-electric power and reclaim fertile cotton-growing land. Nasser played off the two superpowers against each other in an attempt to secure aid for Egyptian economic development. In 1955 he received a shipment of arms from the Soviet bloc. In order to avert an alignment between Egypt and the Soviet Union the United States offered to part-finance the construction of the Aswan Dam. However, Nasser did not entirely sever his ties with the communist world and, when he recognised the People's Republic of China in 1956, the United States cancelled economic aid to Egypt. Nasser aimed to make up for the shortfall in revenue by nationalising the British-owned Suez Canal Company.

Nasser's action brought Anglo-Egyptian relations to the verge of breakdown. France sided with Britain and was keen to bring Nasser down since he was supplying aid to Algerian nationalists fighting against the French in a bloody war of independence. The response of the United

States was to propose an international agreement governing use of the Canal. But the commitment of Britain and France to negotiations was always half-hearted and both were secretly preparing a military operation with Israel to regain the Suez Canal zone. The first military action occurred when Israel invaded the Sinai desert. This was followed by the British bombing of Egyptian airfields and the dropping of British and French paratroops into the Suez Canal zone on 5 November. The Soviet Union immediately branded Britain, France and Israel as 'aggressors' and threatened to intervene militarily in defence of Egypt. At the same time Moscow contacted Washington with a view to a joint US-Soviet military operation against Britain and France. Eisenhower rejected this proposal. He could not side with the Soviet Union against America's allies. The military intervention of both superpowers also risked world war. Nevertheless, he condemned the whole operation. The United States sponsored a resolution in the United Nations, supported by the Soviet Union, for an immediate cease-fire. Under severe diplomatic pressure from the United States, the British, French and Israeli forces withdrew. Eisenhower used America's financial muscle to force a British retreat. In support of Egypt some Arab states had cut oil supplies to Britain. A run on sterling had followed and Ike refused to extend to Britain the dollar credits it needed to purchase oil on the international market. The Anglo-French attempt to recover the Suez Canal zone by force behind the smokescreen of an Israeli invasion of Egypt had failed and the Canal remained under Egypt's control.

Eisenhower opposed the British and French decision to use force for a number of reasons. He was furious at the attempt by the two countries to act without the knowledge of the United States, their major ally. He also calculated that US military intervention on the side of Israel and two colonial powers would have destroyed American efforts to win friends and cement alliances in the Arab world, in addition to inviting the risk of Soviet military action and igniting a major conflict. In the second volume of his presidential memoirs, *Waging Peace* (1965), he provides a further clue to his thinking.

1 At nine o'clock that morning a meeting began with an intelligence review. 'The occurrences in Hungary are a miracle. They have disproved that a popular revolt can't occur in the face of modern weapons. Eighty percent of the Hungarian army has defected.
5 Except in Budapest, even the Soviet troops have shown no stomach for shooting down Hungarians.' The problem in Hungary, he [Foster Dulles] concluded, was the lack of a strong guiding authority for the rebels; Imre Nagy was failing and the rebels were demanding that he resign.
10   Turning to the Middle East, Foster Dulles reviewed the history of recent weeks ... 'It is nothing less than tragic that at this very time, when we are on the point of winning an immense and long

hoped-for victory over Soviet colonialism in Eastern Europe, we
should be forced to choose between following in the footsteps of
15 Anglo-French colonialism in Asia and Africa, or splitting our
course away from their course. Yet this decision must be made in a
mere matter of hours...'
      We could not permit the Soviet Union to seize the leadership in
20 the struggle against the use of force in the Middle East and thus
win the confidence of the new independent nations of the world...

The Suez crisis had several important and long-lasting effects on
American policy. A Soviet-Egyptian alliance emerged in the aftermath
of Suez. The actions of Britain and France pushed Nasser away from the
Western powers and towards Moscow. Nasser's ties to Moscow aroused
new fears about the penetration of Soviet power into the Middle East.
The response was the Eisenhower Doctrine announced in January 1957.
Congress passed a resolution granting the President powers to send
economic or military aid to any Middle Eastern state seeking assistance
against 'overt armed aggression from any nation controlled by
international communism'. Nasser's stock in the Arab world was high
after Suez and pro-Nasser demonstrations occurred in a number of Arab
countries. Because of Nasser's alliance with the Soviet Union some of
these were interpreted by the United States as instances of support for
communism.
      The Eisenhower Doctrine was first invoked in 1957. The King of
Jordan feared a coup by pro-Nasser forces within his country and
appealed to the United States for help. The US Sixth Fleet moved into
the eastern Mediterranean and $10 million in aid was sent to Jordan.
The following year saw the first post-war American military intervention
in the Middle East when 10,000 marines landed on the beaches of
Lebanon in July. The operation was prompted by the apparent growth
of Nasser's influence in the region. Inevitably Washington saw the hand
of Moscow behind such developments. A new United Arab Republic
(Egypt and Syria) had been formed in 1958 and in the Lebanese capital,
Beirut, supporters of Nasser had been protesting against the country's
President, Camille Chamoun. Then the pro-Western Hashemite
monarchy in Iraq was overthrown in a left-wing coup. The landings in
Lebanon could have caused a Cold War crisis. However, in the event,
the Soviet Union limited its actions to diplomatic protests and the US
marines left in October after the election of a new president defused
anti-government protests. The United States also recognised the new
regime in Iraq, even though it had withdrawn from the Baghdad Pact.
The Americans were satisfied that it was not pro-Soviet and that the
Russians had played no part in the overthrow of the Iraqi monarchy.
      American policy in the Middle East under Eisenhower was not an
unqualified success. Admittedly the interests of US oil companies had
been safeguarded and Western access to oil reserves maintained.

Communism had made few advances in the region, but this was due to its limited appeal to the peoples of the Middle East rather than to American actions. Once again the Americans had confused nationalism with communism. Nasser was not a communist and pursued his own nationalist agenda, using Soviet funds to raise his prestige and build Egypt as a regional power. The Baghdad Pact was a weak security organisation. Divisions among Arab states, hostility to the Western powers and the withdrawal of Iraq in 1959 meant that it could never function properly as an anti-Soviet military alliance along the lines of NATO. Israel and some of the smaller Arab states like Lebanon and Jordan may have been US allies, but the hostility of other countries handicapped American efforts to forge alliances in a region which had emerged as a vital area in the Cold War.

ii) Central America and the Caribbean

The United States had always viewed Latin America and the Caribbean as its backyard and was the dominant power in the region. It was an unwritten rule of US policy that communist states must not be allowed to establish themselves so close to America's own borders. Significantly, the first post-war security treaty negotiated by the United States was the Rio Pact in 1947 which stated that an attack against any one country in the Americas would be treated as an attack against all. In 1948 the Organisation of American States (OAS) was formed as the political arm of the Rio Pact. Its charter stipulated that international communism was inconsistent with the 'concept of American freedom'. Both the OAS and the Rio Pact were American-inspired devices to exclude communism from the Western hemisphere.

In 1953 a potential communist threat was identified in Guatemala. The country's president Jacobo Arbenz Guzman had been elected in 1951. Guatemala was a poor country in which 50 per cent of the population lived off only 3 per cent of the land, and one of Arbenz's priorities was land reform. In 1953 he seized unused land owned by the US United Fruit Company. The already suspicious Eisenhower administration saw the seizure of US assets as the prelude to a communist reform programme. The US ambassador's report to Eisenhower after a meeting with Arbenz gives a flavour of the almost hysterical anti-communism of some American policy-makers in this period.

1 It seemed to me that the man thought like a communist, and if not actually one, would do until one came along. I so reported to Secretary Dulles ... and I expressed the view that unless the communist influences in Guatemala were counteracted, Guate-
5 mala would within six months fall completely under Communist control.

There were a smattering of communists in the trade unions and Ministry of Education, but only four in the Guatemalan parliament. Arbenz himself was not a communist nor was he in receipt of aid from Moscow. However, Eisenhower believed that there was sufficient evidence to authorise a CIA plan to overthrow him, Operation PB Success. The man chosen to lead the coup was Castillo Armas, a staunch anti-communist. The CIA supplied him with funds, mercenaries and a base in neighbouring Honduras. Arbenz now attempted to strengthen his position by purchasing a small amount of arms from the Soviet bloc, further proof to the Americans of his communist inclinations.

Armas invaded Guatemala with 150 men in June 1954 and at a crucial juncture Eisenhower agreed to supply him with two planes flown by US pilots. The subsequent bombing of civilian targets led to a collapse of popular support for Arbenz and the defection of his armed forces. He fled to Mexico and after a short interval Armas became president. Armas had suffered only one casualty, but had ordered the massacre of hundreds of political opponents during the coup. Once again a covert CIA operation had deposed a foreign government suspected of links with the Soviet Union and installed a pro-American regime. An anti-communist military dictator served American interests better than a liberal reformer.

The spectre of communism loomed even closer to home when in 1959 Fidel Castro assumed the leadership of the island of Cuba which was only 90 miles from the US mainland. The United States had controlled Cuba since the Spanish-American war of 1898, and since 1934 the island had been ruled by General Fulgencio Batista, an American-sponsored military dictator. Under Batista Cuba was tied closely to the United States both politically and economically. The island was a playground for rich American tourists and most of Cuba's assets were owned by US corporations. In 1956 the forces of the 26th July Movement under the leadership of the Cuban revolutionary Fidel Castro landed on Cuba in an attempt to overthrow Batista. They almost met with immediate defeat, but they retreated into the mountains and established a base of support among the poverty-stricken Cuban peasantry. By 1958 they were winning their war against government forces and on New Year's Day 1959 Castro triumphantly entered the Cuban capital, Havana.

Like Arbenz in Guatemala, Castro quickly initiated a programme of land redistribution. On a visit to the United States he was enthusiastically received and met Vice-President Richard Nixon, who concluded that the revolutionary was not an outright communist. Indeed, most historians believe that Castro only became a Marxist at some point in 1960 or 1961. Nevertheless, Castro's confiscation of US assets on the island and his recognition of communist China aroused American fears that he might become Moscow's newest ally in the Third World. Castro also signed trade agreements with the Soviet Union. Traditionally America had bought Cuba's sugar crop but the Soviet Union now opened its market to Cuban sugar in return for exporting oil and manufactured goods to Cuba. Eisenhower responded with an embargo on Cuban sugar imports and instructed the CIA to train Cuban exiles in Guatemala for an invasion of the island. Castro continued to seize US assets in Cuba and the United States now blocked all trade with Cuba except for a few essential items. In January 1961 the two countries broke off diplomatic relations. The situation in Cuba was one of the difficult problems bequeathed by Ike to his successor, John F. Kennedy, and within two years the small island in the Caribbean would be the scene of the most dangerous US-Soviet confrontation of the Cold War.

4 US-Soviet Relations under Eisenhower

Eisenhower's arrival in the White House and Stalin's death in 1953 produced new Cold War leaders. Yet new leaderships in Washington and Moscow did not bring about a sea-change in US-Soviet relations. Eisenhower and Dulles shared the deep anti-communism of their generation. Cold War attitudes meant that both men found it hard to envisage the Soviet Union as a constructive partner in negotiations. Events on the ground also made a diplomatic breakthrough unlikely. American and Chinese soldiers were killing each other in Korea until July 1953. Eisenhower had to keep an eye on Congress too. Senator McCarthy and his supporters were still riding high and any overture to Moscow would have exposed Ike to accusations of being soft on communism and poisoned relations with both Republicans and Democrats in Congress. The nature of the collective leadership which had succeeded Stalin also made diplomacy difficult. The two leading figures in the Soviet government, Nikita Khrushchev and Georgi Malenkov, were engaged in a power struggle and it was often difficult to know who held the reins of power. It was not until 1957 that Khrushchev emerged as the undisputed leader of the Soviet Union.

One early diplomatic initiative by Eisenhower came to nothing. At the United Nations in 1953 he put forward his 'Atoms for Peace' Plan. Ike proposed that the major powers should deposit a portion of their nuclear stockpiles in a bank of nuclear materials supervised by the UN. The material would then be used for the peaceful generation of nuclear energy. The Russians rejected the plan as a diversionary tactic designed to thwart their own programme of harnessing nuclear energy to military purposes and catching up with the United States in the development of nuclear weapons. Nevertheless, there were signs of a more conciliatory approach to Cold War problems on the part of the Soviet Union. Post-Stalinist Russia was a different kind of enemy. The Russians put pressure on Kim Il Sung to agree to an armistice in Korea in 1953 and persuaded Ho Chi Minh at the Geneva Conference in 1954 to end the war with France and accept the partition of Vietnam as the price of peace. In 1955 the Soviet Union recognised West Germany and in the following year abolished the Cominform. Khrushchev suggested that relations between capitalist and communist states should proceed in a context of 'peaceful co-existence.' He also denounced the crimes of Stalin at the Twentieth Party Congress in 1956. In addition to pursuing a more constructive foreign policy, Russian leaders were relying less on brutality and terror at home.

Agreement on the future of Austria was a further example of improving Soviet-American relations. Like Germany, Austria had been divided into four zones of occupation in 1945. All four powers now agreed to withdraw their occupying forces and unify Austria in return for Austrian neutrality. Austria regained its sovereignty and took its place as a united and neutral state in central Europe. The agreement was initialled in May 1955 and Dulles and the Soviet Foreign Minister Molotov appeared together on a balcony in Vienna. The Austrian State Treaty cleared the way for the Geneva summit later in the same year. Eisenhower sat down with Khrushchev and Bulganin in the first meeting between American and Russian heads of state since the Potsdam Conference in 1945. Little of substance was achieved at the summit and Eisenhower's one concrete proposal was rebuffed by the Russians. On the last day of the summit Ike delivered his 'Open Skies' proposal whereby the Russians and Americans would exchange a blueprint of their military installations and allow mutual aerial inspection of weapons sites. Khrushchev dismissed the plan as a cover for US espionage. There was some truth in this allegation. Since 1954 the Americans had been developing the U-2 reconnaissance plane which was far superior to anything possessed by the Russians. 'Open Skies' would have allowed U-2s to overfly the Soviet Union openly under international agreement. In spite of the absence of tangible results, the Geneva Summit provided an opportunity for dialogue and created a climate of goodwill. There was talk of a 'spirit of Geneva' and at evening parties diplomats joked about 'co-existence cocktails - you know, vodka and Coke'.

The Hungarian rising and the Suez crisis soon dissipated the 'spirit of Geneva'. Tension between Moscow and Washington was accompanied by new fears of the Soviet threat within the United States. Those fears were a reaction to the Russians launching the world's first orbiting satellite, Sputnik. Travelling at 18,000 miles per hour, emitting an electronic signal, and circling the globe every 92 minutes, Sputnik caused panic in the United States. It aroused fears that the Russians would attack the United States from extraterrestrial military bases and convinced many Americans that the Soviet Union was far ahead in guided-missile technology. The governor of Michigan captured the prevailing mood.

Oh little Sputnik
With made-in-Moscow beep,
You tell the world it's a Commie sky
And Uncle Sam's asleep.

Congress and the media fuelled public anxieties. Democrats accused Eisenhower of allowing a dangerous 'missile gap' to grow between the United States and the Soviet Union. Coincidentally a special commission appointed by Ike to examine America's security needs delivered its findings shortly after the launch of Sputnik. The Gaither Report recommended the building of fallout shelters and an increase of $44 billion in defence spending over five years. The newspapers trumpeted the Gaither Report's recommendations and editorialised about the new vulnerability of the United States.

The outcry over Sputnik was a testing time for Eisenhower. His public approval ratings slumped and political opponents accused him of complacency. Yet his response was measured. He rejected the Gaither Report's proposal to bolster defence spending on grounds of cost and dismissed talk of a 'missile gap'. He knew privately that no such gap existed but could not publicly reveal the source of his knowledge. Data from secret U-2 flights conducted since 1956 and subsequently from America's first satellite, *Discoverer,* positioned in August 1960, revealed that the Soviet Union's ballistic weapons programme lagged behind that of the United States. Sputnik showed only that the Russians had the capacity to boost satellites into orbit. In fact the Soviet Union had few usable warheads for their missiles and did not deploy a single ICBM during Ike's period in office. Yet Eisenhower did do something to alleviate public anxiety in the aftermath of Sputnik. He supported the establishment of the National Aeronautics and Space Agency (NASA) in 1958 to oversee missile development and space exploration. Cold War competition now entered a new sphere, outer space. Ike also provided federal aid to promote scientific education in schools under the National Defence Education Act.

Confident in US nuclear superiority, Eisenhower showed a renewed commitment to negotiating with the Soviet Union in the closing period of his presidency. He knew that the United States could bargain from a position of strength. The first substantive issue on which he hoped for progress was a ban on the atmospheric testing of nuclear weapons. America's advantage in this field meant that he could safely contemplate a moratorium on testing. America ceased testing in October 1958 and the Russians immediately followed suit. The prospects for a formal test ban treaty looked good. Soviet-American relations worsened temporarily when Khrushchev issued an ultimatum giving the Americans six months to leave Berlin, but Ike ignored the ultimatum and kept lines of communication to Moscow open. His suggestion of further talks on the issues of Berlin and a test ban led to an agreement by Eisenhower and

Khrushchev to exchange visits. The Russian leader visited the United States briefly in September 1959. As unpredictable as ever, Khrushchev emphasised the importance of friendship while at the same time issuing the boast, 'We will bury you.' Three days spent by Krushchev with Eisenhower at Camp David, the presidential retreat in Maryland, led people to talk of the 'spirit of Camp David'. Plans were laid for a summit in Paris in May 1960 to be followed by a visit to the Soviet Union by Eisenhower. Everything seemed set fair.

Yet the Paris summit collapsed on the first day. On 1 May 1960 a U-2 flown by Gary Powers was shot down over the Soviet Union. Such flights had been going on since 1956. The Russians knew about the flights but could do nothing about them, since the U-2s flew at an altitude which was beyond the range of Soviet fighters and ground-to-air missiles. On three occasions the Soviet Union had protested privately to Washington, but the flights continued. Improved anti-aircraft missiles had enabled the Russians finally to destroy a U-2. Powers himself had ejected and had been captured uninjured by the Russians. He confessed the nature of his mission. Khrushchev now set a trap for the Americans. He announced only that an American plane had been shot down in Soviet airspace. The Eisenhower administration, unwilling to admit publicly that the United States was engaged in espionage, then issued a prepared cover story that the plane was a weather reconnaissance aircraft. Officials assumed that Powers had been killed and that there would be scarcely any evidence of his mission. The Russians then produced Powers and exposed the American version of events as the lie it was, so scoring a propaganda victory. Eisenhower then told the full story, justifying aerial surveillance as a 'distasteful but vital necessity'.

Both leaders turned up in Paris. Khrushchev demanded that Eisenhower condemn U-2 flights and punish those responsible for them. He also cancelled the invitation to the American President to visit the Soviet Union. Eisenhower rejected Khrushchev's demands and agreed only to suspend U-2 flights. The meeting broke up in acrimony. The U-2 incident had scuppered the summit, prevented further progress on the key issues of Berlin and a test ban, and plunged US-Soviet relations to their lowest point under Eisenhower.

One puzzling issue remains: why did Eisenhower sanction the flight at such a delicate moment in East-West relations? A recent American historian of the U-2 incident writing in 1986 offers the following account of the decision-making process behind the flight.

1 [Allen] Dulles and Bissell [Director of U-2 programme] appealed
   for another mission. They wished to get a fresh look at Soviet
   military-industrial landmarks such as Sverdlovsk. But the most
   vital target was six hundred miles north of Moscow at Plesetsk.
5 The April 9 flight had found evidence that the first operational
   ICBMs were being deployed there. Another run would reveal

Soviet progress. Bissell argued that if they waited they might miss the chance to see the missiles under construction. In the northern latitudes the sun's angle was judged critical for U-2 photography.
10 It was argued that a mission over Plesetsk could only be flown effectively from April through July. If they waited until July and the weather was poor, the U-2 might be barred from taking clear pictures of Plesetsk until April 1961.
15   The president was eager to build a lasting detente and knew how each incursion provoked the Russians. Still Khrushchev had not complained of the April flight and had not been able to knock it down. Perhaps it was caution enough to close down the programme for the weeks immediately before the Paris conference.
20 Thus Eisenhower sent the U-2 into the Soviet Union one more time.

Eisenhower himself recalled the decision in his memoirs.

1 We knew that on a number of occasions Soviet fighters scrambled from nearby air bases to attempt interception, but they could never come close enough to damage a U-2. However, I said that while I wholeheartedly approved continuation of the programme, I was
5 convinced in the event of accident we must be prepared for a storm of protest.
   But, with a record of successful flights behind us, the intelligence people became more and more confident that the outcome of each future venture was almost a certainty.
10 Furthermore, the information obtained was important. So when a spring programme for 1960 was proposed, I again approved.

5 Eisenhower and the Cold War: An Assessment

Eisenhower has emerged from recent historiography with an enhanced reputation. Many historians see him as America's finest post-war president and have awarded him high marks for his conduct of foreign policy in the Cold War. In many areas of the world communism was successfully contained. Western Europe, an area vital to the United States, offered a secure frontier against communism. The United States had enlisted West Germany into NATO and its firm stance on the issue of Berlin had prevented the Russians driving the Western powers out of the city. In spite of differences with Britain and France, the US-led alliance in Europe remained intact. In East Asia the doctrine of massive retaliation had helped to deter a Chinese takeover of the Quemoy and Matsu islands and a possible invasion of Taiwan. Nor had there been a significant increase in communist influence on the periphery. In the Middle East America found it difficult to recruit allies among nationalist Arab states, and Moscow's wooing of Nasser showed that the Soviet

Union was a serious competitor for the allegiance of developing Third World nations, but Lebanon and Jordan were US allies in the region in addition to the Jewish state of Israel, and communism had made few significant advances. The CIA-inspired coup in 1953 had also ensured a friendly Iran. Eisenhower's management of the Suez crisis possibly showed him at his most statesmanlike. His opposition to the use of force avoided a major split with Arab states and potential war with the Soviet Union. Ike's response was consistent with his policy of avoiding direct military intervention wherever possible. Only once, in the Lebanon, did he send US armed forces into action during his presidency. Elsewhere on the periphery CIA action in Guatemala eliminated a perceived communist threat.

Eisenhower also deserves some credit for controlling the costs of the Cold War. Between 1953 and 1959 he reduced the size of the US Army by 671,000, and total defence spending in his first term fell from $50.4 billion in 1953 to $40.3 billion in 1959. Military spending rose to $46.6 billion in 1959, but Ike steadfastly refused the massive increases demanded by the public and political opponents alike in the late 1950s, while maintaining American nuclear superiority, The same strategic superiority only reinforced his genuine commitment to negotiations with the Soviet Union. His diplomacy ultimately failed, but Soviet-American relations were often warmer under Eisenhower than they had been in any previous phase of the Cold War.

On the debit side, the Eisenhower administration's policy in Indochina was a failure. The decision not to participate in elections in 1956 suggested that the United States supported the principle of free elections only so long as the likely victors were not communists. President Diem was a corrupt and repressive ruler. His regime did not command the support of substantial sections of the South Vietnamese population nor was it capable of resisting communist insurgency. The government installed by the Americans in neighbouring Laos proved equally vulnerable to internal communist opposition.

While policy-makers at the time believed that CIA actions in Iran and Guatemala pre-empted the entry of those states into the Soviet orbit, the verdict of historians has been harsher. The overthrow of Mossadeq and Arbenz rested on the false assumption that nationalist and reforming leaders in the world's emerging nations were likely to be communist fellow-travellers. The coups in both countries have been seen as among the worst examples of American imperialism in the Cold War era. Arguably Eisenhower's reliance on covert CIA operations made the agency too powerful, unaccountable not only to Congress but to the President himself. Unknown to Eisenhower the CIA was laying plans for the assassination of Castro and other communist leaders in 1960. Probably Eisenhower's greatest failure occurred in the last year of his presidency. His authorisation of a U-2 flight on the eve of the Paris summit was a major error of judgement and destroyed his cherished ambition of achieving a permanent thaw between Moscow and Washington. Indeed Eisenhower left his young successor, John Kennedy, a difficult legacy: unresolved problems in Laos, Vietnam and Cuba and a crisis in US-Soviet relations. It would not take the inexperienced Kennedy long to find out just how problematic his inheritance was.

Making notes on *'Co-existence and Confrontation: Eisenhower's Cold War, 1953-61'*

Use the end-of-chapter summary diagram and the chapter headings to give structure to your notes. When you start making notes on the chapter, approach the material with the following question in mind. What was the purpose of the 'New Look'? It might then be a good idea to make a list of the similarities and differences between Truman's and Eisenhower's policies of containment. Make sure that your notes cover how containment was applied in practice under Eisenhower. Consider each of the major regions of the world separately. You might also organise the information on each region into the successes and failures of the policy of containment. In this way you will avoid a mass of detail and your notes will have an analytical framework. Next you should examine Eisenhower's record in the field of US-Soviet relations. Once again you might wish to distinguish between his successes and his failures. At the end of your notes you should compile an assessment of Eisenhower, citing his strengths and weaknesses as a Cold War leader. Such an assessment should reflect your own opinion and attempt to measure what Eisenhower achieved against what his aims were.

Answering essay questions on *'Co-existence and Confrontation: Eisenhower's Cold War, 1953-61'*

Eisenhower and the Cold War is a very broad topic. The following essay questions indicate the areas on which your understanding might be tested.

1   Compare Eisenhower's and Truman's policies of containment.
2   By what means and with what success did the United States contain communism in *either* Indochina *or* the Middle East *or* Latin America during Eisenhower's presidency?
3   Analyse US policy towards China under Eisenhower.
4   'A series of missed opportunities.' Evaluate this judgement of Eisenhower's handling of US-Soviet relations.

In question 1 the instruction word is 'compare'. 'Compare' is asking you to consider things in relation to each other, emphasising similarities and differences. What aspects of Truman's and Eisenhower's policies of containment should you be investigating? This might best be done by

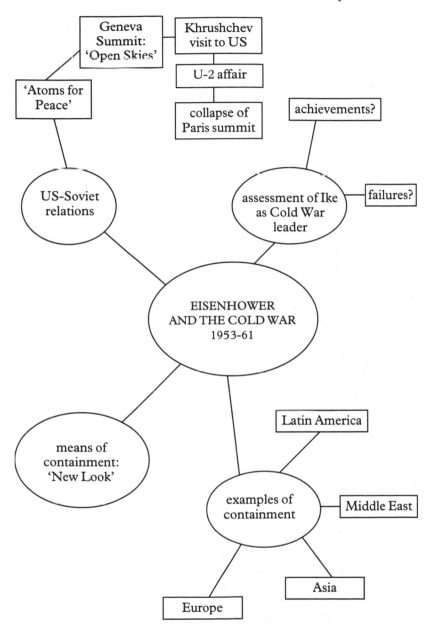

Summary - Co-existence and Confrontation: Eisenhower's Cold War, 1953-61

thinking in terms of a comparison of aims and methods. You might draw up a simple table of similarities and differences between Truman's and Eisenhower's policies under those sub-headings. Such a table might form your plan and the basis of your essay. Firstly, tackle similarities, then differences.

For question 2 you must first choose the area of the world you are going to discuss. Then examine the methods employed by the United States to contain communism in that region. This part of your essay will largely be descriptive. Next comes the analysis. 'With what success' invites you to consider successful examples of containment in the region of the world under discussion, but you should also be willing to mention failures. Only then will your response to the question be balanced.

Question 3 is a broad and open-ended question. The issue under discussion is US policy towards China and the time-frame is 1953-60. The advantage of this question is that within those limits you can more or less set your own terms of reference. 'Analyse' is our cue word. To analyse a topic is to study it in depth and to describe and explain its main characteristics. In a question of this sort it is easy just to narrate. You can avoid a purely descriptive answer by focusing on particular aspects of US policy towards China. For example, you might consider the goals, methods and outcomes of policy, examining how far the outcomes fulfilled the goals. You might also want to cite and explain changes in policy.

Question 4 is an altogether different type of question. In inverted commas you are given a hypothesis or proposition and you have to decide how well that hypothesis fits Eisenhower's conduct of US-Soviet relations. You are asked to 'evaluate' the hypothesis, which means you have to consider its worth and pinpoint its advantages and limitations. In the first part of your answer you might give examples of missed opportunities for which Eisenhower was to blame. A striking instance was the Paris summit in 1960. On the other side of the argument you might give examples of Eisenhower's role in improving US-Soviet relations. Think about the Geneva summit in 1955 and the invitation to Khrushchev to tour the United States in 1959. On this side of the argument you might also point out that not all the failures in US-Soviet diplomacy were attributable to Eisenhower. Until 1955 it was not clear which member of the Soviet leadership exercised real power. Subsequently Eisenhower had to contend with a difficult and unpredictable opponent.

Source-based questions on '*Co-existence and Confrontation: Eisenhower's Cold War, 1953-61*'

1 Cartoon, 1958
Examine the visual source on page 80 and answer the following questions.
a) Identify the two key figures in the cartoon. (2 marks)
b) Which historical event might have been the occasion for the appearance of this cartoon? (1 mark)
c) 'The cartoonist presents an essentially favourable view of brinkmanship'. Do you agree? Explain your answer. (7 marks)

2 Suez Crisis, 1956
Read the extract on pages 92-3 and answer the following questions.
a) In the context of the extract explain the following terms. i) 'the occurrences in Hungary' (lines 2); (1 mark) ii) 'Soviet colonialism' (line 13); (1 mark) iii) 'Anglo-French colonialism' (line 15) (1 mark)
b) Does this source fully explain why the United States did not use force during the Suez Crisis? Explain your answer. (7 marks)

3 U-2 Affair
Read the extracts on pages 99-100 and answer the following questions.
a) In the context of the extract explain the following terms.
   i) 'operational ICBMs' (lines 5-6); (1 mark) ii) 'the Paris Conference' (line 17); (1 mark)
b) How far do the two sources agree about the reasons for the U-2 flight in May 1960? (3 marks)
c) Which of the two sources might be more reliable as evidence about why Eisenhower decided to authorise the U-2 flight in May 1960? Explain your answer. (5 marks)

CHAPTER 6

Crisis and Compromise: Kennedy's Cold War, 1961-3

1 Introduction

John F. Kennedy assumed the presidency of the United States after a narrow victory over Richard Nixon in the 1960 presidential election. He was born in 1917 into a rich Boston Irish-American family and educated at private schools and Harvard University. From an early age he was familiar with the world of high politics. His father, Joseph Kennedy, who had made his money in banking and business, was US ambassador to Britain between 1938 and 1940. The son achieved success early in life. He travelled in pre-war Europe and in 1940 wrote a best-seller, *Why England Slept,* a critical analysis of Britain's policy of appeasement in the 1930s. During his war service he was decorated for his actions after his torpedo boat was sunk by the Japanese and he rescued some of his fellow sailors. Backed by his father's money, the ambitious Kennedy then enjoyed a rapid rise in post-war national politics. The state of Massachusetts was his political power-base. He won a seat in Congress in 1946 and entered the Senate in 1952.

In the late 1940s and 1950s Kennedy had been a dedicated Cold Warrior. He had bemoaned the 'loss' of China and spoken in support of McCarthy at the height of the 'Red scare'. Later he criticised Eisenhower for allowing a 'missile gap' to develop between the United States and the Soviet Union. A speech in September 1960 during the presidential election campaign was typical of his views.

1 The enemy is the communist system itself - implacable, insatiable, increasing in its drive for world domination ... This is not a struggle for supremacy of arms alone. It is also a struggle for supremacy between two conflicting ideologies: freedom under
5 God versus ruthless, godless tyranny.

During the election he cultivated the image of a man of action. He emphasised his dynamism and willingness to take decisions. He promised Americans that he would regain the initiative in the Cold War. Kennedy took up the theme in his eloquent inaugural address to the American people. He sent a clear message both to Americans and to the Kremlin.

Let every nation know, whether it wishes us well or ill, that we shall pay any price, bear any burden, meet any hardship, oppose any foe to assure the survival and success of liberty.

Kennedy's choice of personnel as president reflected his anti-communist sentiments. The equally anti-communist Dean Rusk was appointed Secretary of State. In particular, Rusk was vehemently anti-Chinese and opposed any rapprochement with the People's Republic of China. The new National Security Adviser, McGeorge Bundy, and Secretary of Defence, Robert McNamara, were also Cold Warriors. The Kennedy-Rusk relationship was very different from that between Eisenhower and Dulles. No real rapport existed between Kennedy and his Secretary of State and the President more often depended on Bundy, McNamara and other advisers. Indeed the whole process of decision-making was more streamlined in the Kennedy administration. Ike had relied heavily on the State Department and sessions of the National Security Council, whereas Kennedy tended to short-circuit the State Department and slimmed down the NSC. The new President's preferred system of policy-making was to talk issues through informally with a small circle of trusted advisers and then reach a decision.

Like previous presidents and mindful of the party political divisions of Truman's later years, Kennedy attempted to build bipartisan support for his foreign policy in Congress. Important posts in Kennedy's administration were not held exclusively by Democrats. Bundy and McNamara, for example, were both Republicans. The results of the 1960 Congressional elections also favoured the new President. The Democrats had a majority in both houses of Congress which survived the mid-term elections in 1962. Democrat control of both the executive and the legislature lessened the chances of conflict between President and Congress over foreign policy issues.

2 Containment under Kennedy: Flexible Response

The strategy of containment employed under Kennedy was called 'flexible response'. Its main elements were an increase in conventional forces, the enlargement of the nuclear arsenal, economic aid, covert action and negotiations with the Soviet Union. The central purpose of 'flexible response' was to expand the available means of countering communism. This versatile strategy rested on the premise that the communist threat was now more diverse than it had ever been. The United States must have the capacity both to fight a limited conventional war in Europe or Asia and to retaliate against a nuclear strike by the Soviet Union. At the same time America must have the means to combat revolutionary movements in the Third World backed by the Soviet Union or China. As soon as Kennedy had entered the White House, Khrushchev had promised that the Russians would champion wars of national liberation. Flexible response was therefore a reaction to the new tactics of the communist powers and the expansion of the Cold War into new areas of the world. It was also a deliberate departure from Eisenhower's policy of deterring communist gains by threatening to use nuclear weapons. One of the inherent risks of the doctrine of 'massive retaliation' was that it left the president with very few options if an opponent did not give in to nuclear blackmail. In July 1961 Kennedy himself put the point succinctly, 'We intend to have a wider choice than humiliation or all-out nuclear war.'

A strategy of containment based on enlarging both conventional and nuclear forces was obviously costly, but was permitted by the different economic policies pursued by Kennedy. Eisenhower's economic policy revolved around balanced budgets and tight control of government expenditure. Kennedy, on the other hand, pursued an expansionist economic policy based on higher levels of federal spending and budget deficits. The new President and his advisers believed that federal spending on defence would stimulate output, employment and consumption and benefit the overall economy. Military spending grew by 13 per cent under Kennedy. The defence budget rose from $47.4 billion in 1961 to $53.6 in 1964.

There were clear differences between Eisenhower's and Kennedy's conceptions of containment. The New Look emphasised nuclear weapons at the expense of conventional forces; flexible response committed the United States both to continued modernisation and expansion of its nuclear arsenal and to strengthening its conventional capabilities. In this respect it was reminiscent of the strategy of containment outlined in NSC 68 in 1950. The cuts in conventional forces imposed by Ike were reversed by Kennedy. The number of combat-ready divisions increased from 11 to 16 and the armed forces grew in size from 2.5 million men in 1960 to 2.7 million men in 1964. The growth of the armed forces included an increase in the number of soldiers trained in techniques of counter-insurgency warfare - so called 'special forces' such as the Green Berets. Such troops could be deployed to fight against communist-backed guerrilla forces in the developing world.

Kennedy also attached more importance than Eisenhower to economic aid as an instrument of containment. In his inaugural address he made it clear that economic assistance to new nations was based on a mixture of idealism and a self-interested attempt to minimise communist influence.

1 To those new states whom we welcome to the ranks of the free, we
  pledge our word that one form of colonial control shall not have
  passed away merely to be replaced by a far more iron tyranny. We
  shall not always expect to find them supporting our own view. But
5 we shall always hope to find them strongly supporting their own
  freedom, and to remember that, in the past, those who foolishly
  sought power by riding the back of the tiger ended up inside.
    To those people in the huts and villages of half the globe
  struggling to break the bonds of mass misery, we pledge our best

10 efforts to help them help themselves … not because the
communists may be doing it, not because we seek their votes, but
because it is right.

The United States wanted to offer a model of political and economic
development to emerging nations which was different from communism. Dollar subsidies would create economically viable and more or less
democratic states in the developing world beyond the reach of Soviet
influence. The ousting of communist regimes in the Third World under
Eisenhower had tackled the symptoms but not the causes of
communism. Kennedy wanted to remove the economic conditions
which created the seed-bed for communism. In an attempt to alleviate
poverty in Latin America the Alliance for Progress was founded in 1961
and $20 billion was set aside to promote living standards by reforms
such as land redistribution. A Peace Corps of volunteers was formed to
work on health, educational and agricultural projects in the Third World
and an Agency for International Development targeted overseas aid at
developing countries.

However, the continuity between Kennedy's and Eisenhower's
policies of containment was as marked as the change. The new President
soon discovered that no 'missile gap' existed, but the accumulation of
nuclear missiles continued in order to preserve US strategic superiority.
ten new Polaris submarines were built (America now had 29) and 400
additional Minuteman missiles were constructed, taking the total to
800. Kennedy's announcement of the Apollo space programme in 1961
also exemplified his commitment to maintaining strategic superiority.
He wanted the United States to enjoy an advantage over the Soviet
Union not only in the quantity and quality of its nuclear arsenal but in
the exploration of outer space. He promised that the Americans would
be the first to put a man on the moon and after the expenditure of
between $25 and $35 billion his promise was fulfilled in 1969.

Covert actions were also an important aspect of containment under
Kennedy. In 1961 the CIA planned an invasion of Cuba by anti-Castro
Cuban exiles and subsequently implemented Operation Mongoose,
whose objective was to destabilise Castro's communist regime in Cuba
and ultimately to bring down the Cuban leader. A further important
similarity between Ike and his successor was Kennedy's willingness to
negotiate with the Russians, signalled in his inaugural address.

1 Finally, to those nations who would make themselves our
adversary, we offer not a pledge but a request: that both sides begin
anew the quest for peace, before the dark powers of destruction
unleashed by science engulf all humanity in planned or accidental
5 self-destruction … Let us never negotiate out of fear, but let us
never fear to negotiate.

During Kennedy's presidency there were moments of crisis in US-Soviet relations but bilateral diplomacy continued and agreements were reached on specific issues. There were, however, no comparable negotiations with communist China. The United States continued to withhold diplomatic recognition from the People's Republic of China and to oppose its admission to the United Nations. Several factors precluded a warmer Sino-American relationship. Important pressure groups within the United States still opposed the recognition of China, while policy-makers were also worried about the growth of Chinese influence in south-east Asia and particularly evidence of Chinese aid to Ho's government in North Vietnam. Finally, the Chinese themselves showed little interest in improving relations with the Americans. Mao was firmly opposed to any form of detente (relaxation of tension) with the United States.

3 Indochina: A Case Study in Flexible Response

a) Laos

Laos confronted Kennedy with the first Cold War crisis of his presidency. Between 1955 and 1960 the Eisenhower administration had poured $300 million in aid into the country in an attempt to defeat the communist Pathet Lao forces. In 1958 the CIA had installed a pro-Western government in Laos under General Phoumi Nosavan. But Eisenhower's plan to convert Laos into a bulwark against communism in south-east Asia was frustrated by an on-going civil war in which the Pathet Lao joined with other opposition forces against the government. They continued to gain territory and were receiving substantial aid from both North Vietnam and the Soviet Union.

In March 1961 Kennedy held a press conference with maps illustrating the extent of the Pathet Lao advance and protested at Soviet intervention in Laos. The new President was determined to exclude the Soviet Union from all parts of south-east Asia. The basis of American policy in the region was a non-communist South Vietnam, and a communist takeover of Laos would open South Vietnam to communist infiltration. Kennedy now threatened US military intervention in an attempt to stop Soviet assistance to the Pathet Lao. The Seventh Fleet was despatched to the Gulf of Thailand and US forces in the Far East were put on alert. The United States also secured promises of military support from several members of SEATO. At this point Khrushchev, judging that Laos was an area of only marginal importance to the Soviet Union, agreed to a cease-fire and in 1962 both superpowers settled the conflict by negotiation. In Geneva they signed an agreement guaranteeing Laotian neutrality.

Kennedy's plans to use military force in Laos appeared to have ended Soviet interference in the country. But in fact the agreement in Geneva merely marked the beginning of an unofficial war. The Russians continued to supply the Pathet Lao and the Americans resorted to secret operations. Thirty thousand Laotian Meo tribesmen and 17,000 Thai mercenaries were organised by the CIA into an anti-communist guerrilla force and CIA-operated Air America planes bombed Pathet Lao strongholds. Yet covert action did not prevent further gains by the Pathet Lao. The attempt to contain communism in Laos under Kennedy by both negotiation and undercover action had failed.

b) Vietnam

After the Laotian crisis the focus of US policy in Indochina shifted to Vietnam. Kennedy shared the assumptions of his predecessors about Vietnam. He described the country as the 'cornerstone of the free world in south-east Asia'. He was an adherent of the domino theory: the communist takeover of South Vietnam would expose the states of Indonesia and Malaysia to communist influence. The rice-bowl of south-east Asia would fall under communist control and the United States would forfeit overseas bases. The geopolitical importance of Vietnam was never questioned by Kennedy nor by any member of his administration. The survival of an independent non-communist Vietnam was an article of faith.

Policy-makers were convinced that communist China and the Soviet Union were directing communist insurgency in the south. Vietnam was part of a larger struggle between the United States and the communist powers for hegemony in south-east Asia. A victory for the communists in South Vietnam would in turn tilt the global power balance in favour of the Russians and Chinese. In this sense Vietnam was truly a Cold War issue. The following report to Kennedy by Defence Secretary McNamara was representative of views within Washington.

> 1 The fall of South Vietnam to Communism would lead to the fairly
> rapid extension of Communist control, or complete accommoda-
> tion to Communism, in the rest of mainland Southeast Asia and in
> Indonesia. The strategic implications worldwide, particularly in
> 5 the Orient, would be extremely serious.

Kennedy's policy in Vietnam differed from Eisenhower's only in degree. He increased economic aid to South Vietnam and despatched additional military advisers, but he opposed sending US troops into combat. He wanted to reconcile the twin objectives of rescuing South Vietnam from communism and of avoiding entanglement in a limited war similar to the Korean conflict. Twice in 1961 he rejected advice to commit US ground troops. After a visit to Vietnam Kennedy's Vice-President, Lyndon Johnson, recommended sending a limited number of troops and later the Taylor-Rostow report suggested deploying 8,000 soldiers

in the guise of a flood relief team. Kennedy outlined his policy in
Vietnam to Walter Cronkite on national television in September 1963.

1 *Cronkite:* Mr President, the only hot war we've got running at the
   moment is of course the one in Vietnam and we have our
   difficulties there quite obviously.
   Kennedy: I don't think that unless a greater effort is made by the
5 government to win popular support that the war can be won out
   there. In the final analysis, it is their war. They are the ones who
   have to win it or lose it. We can help them, we can give them
   equipment, we can send our men out there as advisers, but they
   have to win it, the people of Vietnam, against the Communists.
10 *Cronkite:* Hasn't every indication from Saigon been that President
   Diem has no intention of changing his pattern?
   Kennedy: If he does not change it, of course, that is his decision.
   Our best judgement is that he can't be successful on this basis. We
   hope that he comes to see that, but in the final analysis it is the
15 people and the government itself who have to win or lose this
   struggle. All we can do is help, but I don't agree with those who say
   we should withdraw. That would be a great mistake. I know people
   don't like Americans to be engaged in this kind of an effort, but this
   is a very important struggle even though it is very far away. We took
20 all this - made this effort to defend Europe. Now Europe is quite
   secure. We also have to participate - we may not like it - in the
   defence of Asia.

Communist opposition from within South Vietnam was the major
threat to America interests. In the countryside South Vietnamese
communists had organised themselves into guerrilla units. They were
called Vietcong (Vietnam communists - a term of abuse coined by
Diem). They initiated a campaign of terrorism against Diem's
government. By 1961 4,000 government officials a year were being
assassinated. There is no evidence of direct Chinese or Soviet support
for the Vietcong, but they were backed by Ho Chi Minh's communist
regime in North Vietnam. In 1959 the communists in the north had
pledged themselves to the reunification of Vietnam by armed struggle.
Under instructions from Hanoi the southern communists formed the
National Liberation Front (NLF) in 1960. The NLF was the political
wing of the Vietcong and its functions were to co-ordinate resistance
and to act as an umbrella organisation for the diverse groups opposing
Diem in the south. Ho's government now assumed a wider role in the
conflict in the south. The Vietcong received money and supplies from
the north delivered along a conduit known as the Ho Chi Minh trail
which partly ran through neighbouring Laos. Ho was also sending
back former members of the communist Vietminh who had lived in
the south before the division of Vietnam along the 17th parallel in

1954 to train and organise the guerrillas in the south.

One of Kennedy's military advisers offered the following assessment of the threat posed by communist insurgency in Vietnam in November 1961.

> Communist strategy aims to gain control of Southeast Asia by methods of subversion and guerrilla war which by-pass conventional US and indigenous strength on the ground. This strategy is well on the way to success in Vietnam.

Kennedy's response to the growing penetration of rural areas by the Vietcong was threefold. He increased the number of US military advisers, authorised counter-insurgency operations against the communist guerrillas in the south, and pressed Diem to enact reforms. Kennedy doubled the number of military advisers to 2,000 in 1961. The following year the figure grew to 11,000, supported by 300 aircraft and 120 helicopters, and by the end of 1963 there were 16,000 military advisers on the ground in Vietnam. American pilots were flying South Vietnamese soldiers in and out of battle and occasionally US soldiers in self-defence engaged in direct combat with the Vietcong. A hundred US soldiers had died in Vietnam by the end of Kennedy's presidency. Counter-insurgency measures included 'search and destroy' missions against Vietcong units in the countryside and the spraying of defoliants such as Agent Orange in order to deprive Vietcong soldiers of cover in the jungle. The Americans also implemented the strategic hamlet programme. South Vietnamese villagers were resettled in fortified compounds and educated in American values. The idea was to isolate the peasantry from the Vietcong and create strongholds in rural areas.

Vietnam was a testing-ground for the strategy of flexible response. By 1963, however, the strategy was clearly failing. The commitment of additional resources and the resort to different tactics had not contained communism in South Vietnam. The counter-insurgency measures adopted against the Vietcong were themselves flawed. The concentration of peasants in strategic hamlets was unpopular. It compelled ordinary Vietnamese to leave their villages and ancient burial grounds, and the hamlets were not impervious to infiltration by the Vietcong, who were indistinguishable from ordinary peasants. To some extent the Americans were operating against an invisible enemy. 'Search and destroy' missions were only partially effective. A village apparently restored to government control by day was often overrun by the Vietcong at night. The use of the chemical napalm also devastated large parts of the countryside and contributed to rapidly growing support for the Vietcong in late 1962. The inflow of American dollars had created a class of corrupt officials and army officers more interested in making money than in fighting the Vietcong. Most importantly perhaps, the man chosen by the Americans to lead South Vietnam, President Diem, was deeply unpopular. His failure to implement a proper programme of land reform had left the peasantry dissatisfied. The Americans discovered that military operations against communist guerrillas were no substitute for the sort of political and economic reconstruction which might have prevented the discontent so cleverly exploited by the Vietcong in the countryside.

The open discrimination against Buddhists and the ruthless suppression of opposition by a secret police force under Diem's brother, Ngo Dinh Nhu, had also antagonised many South Vietnamese. Diem had very little support outside the Catholic minorities in the cities and in the summer of 1963 support for his regime collapsed. Buddhists staged massive demonstrations and were fired upon by government forces. In Saigon a Buddhist monk set fire to himself in protest. When Diem's sister-in-law described his action as a 'barbecue show', even staunch supporters of Diem in the United States began to question their continuing commitment to South Vietnam's president. These doubts were shared by Kennedy. Against a background of rising unrest the CIA with Kennedy's knowledge encouraged army generals to overthrow Diem. In November the Americans deposed the man they had chosen to lead South Vietnam. The coup was a measure of the failure of US policy. Both Diem and his brother were killed. On hearing the news, Kennedy was shocked. He had intended only to have Diem displaced. A few weeks later the president himself was dead.

4 Kennedy v. Khrushchev 1: The Berlin Crisis, 1961

In June 1961 Kennedy and Khrushchev held a summit in Vienna. The Soviet leader was a difficult adversary. He could be conciliatory at one moment and aggressive the next. Kennedy suspected that Khrushchev would try to exploit his relative inexperience in foreign affairs. His great fear was humiliation at the hands of the Soviet leader. Consequently he regarded the meeting with Khrushchev as a test of his mettle and planned carefully for their summit. 'I'll have to show him that we can be as tough as he is ... I'll have to sit down and let him see who he is dealing with', he observed before leaving for Vienna.

One of the key issues at the summit was the future of Berlin. Since 1958 Khrushchev had been seeking a new Berlin settlement and he now reopened the issue. He told Kennedy that unless Western forces withdrew from the city, the Soviet Union would conclude a separate peace treaty with East Germany. Such a treaty would terminate the post-war rights of the Western powers in Berlin and allow East Germany to close off the air, road and rail corridors to West Berlin. It was a typically aggressive initiative from Khrushchev, but it was also an admission of weakness. Berlin represented a chink in the iron curtain. Many East Germans were exploiting the freedom of movement between the eastern and western sectors of the city permitted by post-war agreements. Once in West Berlin they escaped to the West via the Berlin corridor. In particular, the haemorrhage of skilled labour was hurting the East German economy and Khrushchev wanted to halt the damaging exodus of refugees. Kennedy's response to Khrushchev's threat was unyielding. He stated that the presence of Western troops in the city was non-negotiable. The reasons for the American commitment to Berlin had not changed. The city was an outpost of the 'free world' in the Soviet bloc. A retreat from Berlin would be a blow to US prestige and encourage Khrushchev to seek further concessions elsewhere.

The summit broke up without an agreement on Berlin or any other issue. Kennedy warned Khrushchev that it would be a cold winter. As soon as Kennedy returned to the United States, the Soviet leader issued a six-month deadline for the withdrawal of Western troops from Berlin. Kennedy's response was tough. He asked Congress for an increase in defence spending, put 120,000 reservists on standby and called for a programme to build fallout shelters in case of nuclear war with the Soviet Union. The President also sent an unambiguous message to the Kremlin that the United States would stand firm on the Berlin issue, announcing that 'we cannot and will not allow the Communists to drive us out of Berlin either gradually or by force'.

In August the Berlin crisis entered a new phase. The uncertainty over the future of the city had accelerated the flow of refugees from East Germany. On 12 August alone 4,000 refugees had fled to the West and on the following day the East German government began to seal off the eastern part of the city to prevent further East Germans escaping. Barbed wire fences were erected along the boundary between the eastern and western sectors of the city. These fences were later strengthened to form the Berlin Wall. The Americans immediately despatched a force of 1,500 men to Berlin to establish that access to the city remained open. At the German border Soviet and East German soldiers let them pass unhindered. There was also no interference with the rail and air corridors. Tension mounted when the US commander in Berlin moved tanks equipped with bulldozer blades to the site of the Wall, while on the other side Soviet tanks moved into position. A classic Cold War confrontation ensued until both sides agreed to withdraw. But in the end the Berlin crisis did not erupt into war. The Americans saw the construction of the Berlin Wall as a defensive measure which did not threaten the interests of the Western powers in Berlin. The Russians also did not want to go to war over Berlin. Having achieved his primary objective of closing off an avenue of escape to the West, Khrushchev abandoned his attempt to force the Western powers out of the city. In October the Soviet Union withdrew its ultimatum for the withdrawal of Western troops and Berlin remained a Western enclave within communist Europe for the remainder of the Cold War. The Russians never again tried to revise the post-war settlement of Berlin and the status of the city ceased to be a major issue in US-Soviet relations.

Kennedy's firm diplomacy in the summer of 1961 had paid dividends. He had demonstrated that Khrushchev could not intimidate him into making concessions and had secured the future of West Berlin.

4 Kennedy v. Khrushchev 2: The Cuban Missile Crisis, 1962

a) Origins

Kennedy shared Eisenhower's hostility to Fidel Castro's regime in Cuba. He did not object to the Cuban revolution in itself. What he could not accept was Castro's friendship with Moscow, which represented an unwelcome intrusion of communist influence into the Western hemisphere. The new President inherited a secret plan prepared by the CIA to topple Castro. There was a large community of expatriate Cubans in the United States who had fled the island when Castro seized power. Equipped and financed by the Americans, these anti-Castro exiles were being trained to invade Cuba and overthrow the Cuban leader in a counter-revolution. Some members of Kennedy's administration, Rusk for example, harboured doubts about such an operation, but Kennedy approved the invasion plan. He had criticised Eisenhower's passive policy towards Castro and had accused him of 'losing' Cuba. He now had a chance early in his presidency to demonstrate that he was tough on communism. His decision was also consistent with the view at the time that the United States had the right to overthrow hostile regimes so close to home. The Americans had removed Arbenz in Guatemala in 1954 by covert action and would now do the same to Castro.

The invasion force landed at the Bay of Pigs on 17 April 1961 and was easily defeated by the Cuban army and air force. The whole exercise was ill-fated. Preliminary raids by CIA-operated bombers had inflicted little damage. The exiles were handicapped by a shortage of ammunition and a lack of air cover. Poor intelligence played a part too. Coral reefs incorrectly identified on photographs by the CIA as seaweed punctured landing vessels. There was also no spontaneous uprising against Castro. The Bay of Pigs invasion was a humiliating rebuff for Kennedy and handed Castro an easy propaganda victory. Kennedy salvaged some credibility when he took full responsibility for the operation in a television broadcast, but he never trusted the CIA to the same extent again.

The United States still wanted to overthrow Castro but now had to resort to a different strategy. American policy towards Cuba after the Bay of Pigs invasion was a classic example of flexible response. Washington attempted to weaken Castro's regime by a programme of covert action (Operation Mongoose), economic and diplomatic isolation of Cuba, and military pressure. American agents sabotaged petroleum installations on the island, while the CIA sank Cuban merchant vessels in the Caribbean. The United States maintained a strict embargo on all Cuban imports and secured Cuba's expulsion from the Organisation of American States (OAS) in 1962. Meanwhile 40,000 US troops practised amphibious invasions near Puerto Rico as a reminder to Castro of the military might of the United States.

Castro's response was to request further military aid from the Soviet Union. By 1962 there were 42,000 Russian troops on Cuba equipped with short-range tactical nuclear weapons. The Russians also began to build sites for ballistic missiles on the island. The construction of missile sites was partly a response to Castro's demands for additional protection. In this sense the aggressive policy of the United States towards Cuba was a cause of the Cuban missile crisis. Castro's appeal to the Soviet Union for protection was rational in view of the Bay of Pigs invasion and subsequent American efforts to destabilise his government. Recently declassified sources suggest that the Russians also wanted to instal missiles on Cuba as a defensive measure to deter an American invasion. However, in his memoirs, published in 1970, Khrushchev suggests that the Soviet Union had other motives.

1 I had the idea of installing missiles with nuclear warheads in Cuba without letting the United States find out they were there until it was too late to do anything about them. My thinking went like this: if we installed the missiles secretly and then if the United States
5 discovered the missiles were there after they were already poised and ready to strike, the Americans would think twice before trying to liquidate our installations by military means. In addition to protecting Cuba, our missiles would have equalised what the West likes to call 'the balance of power'. The Americans had surrounded
10 our country with missile bases and threatened us with nuclear weapons, and now they would learn just what it feels like to have enemy missiles pointing at you.

b) Course

Timetable of a Crisis

14 Oct.	Kennedy saw U-2 photographs of missile sites and launch pads on Cuba
16 Oct.	Kennedy assembled ExComm group of advisers
22 Oct.	Kennedy announced 'quarantine' on national television
24 Oct.	Soviet ships carrying warheads turned back in face of blockade
26 Oct.	Khrushchev sent his first telegram: removal of missiles in return for non-invasion pledge
	U-2 shot down over Cuba
27 Oct.	Khrushchev sent his second telegram stating removal of US Jupiter missiles in Turkey as condition of withdrawal of

Soviet missiles from Cuba
US offered non-invasion pledge in return for dismantling of
Soviet missiles
Robert Kennedy met Dobrynin and offered private
assurances about later removal of Jupiters

28 Oct.   Khrushchev agreed to withdraw missiles in return for
non-invasion commitment

On 14 October 1962 Kennedy examined U-2 photographs which offered incontrovertible evidence that launch pads for medium- and intermediate-range ballistic missiles were being constructed by the Russians on Cuba. He now faced the gravest crisis of his presidency. For the next fortnight the world lived in fear of a nuclear war between the superpowers. Kennedy was determined that the missiles should be withdrawn. They represented a major threat to national security, since Cuba was only 90 miles away from Florida. IRBMs had a range of 1,000 miles and would give the Russians the capacity to strike cities deep within the United States. Other considerations also influenced Kennedy. If America allowed the Soviet Union to deploy missiles on Cuba, then the Russians would probe elsewhere. Weakness in one place was symptomatic of weakness elsewhere. In particular, the President was worried about a Soviet takeover of West Berlin. The lesson of appeasement in the 1930s was always a powerful factor in Kennedy's thinking. British and French concessions to Hitler had not avoided further German aggression. American concessions to the Russians now would only encourage a further advance in Soviet power. Kennedy also saw Khrushchev's placement of missiles on Cuba as a further test of his character by the Soviet leader. At one level the Cuban missile crisis was a personal confrontation.

Kennedy gathered a small group of advisers around him to deal with the crisis. They were given the name of the Executive Committee of the National Security Council (ExComm). The initial debate within ExComm centred on two possible responses to Soviet actions: a naval blockade of Cuba or an air strike against the missile sites. The military members of ExComm favoured surgical air strikes against the sites and were supported by some of the civilian advisers. But at the last minute Kennedy ignored the advice of the 'hawks' and decided in favour of a blockade. The purpose of the blockade was to prevent warheads and other components necessary for the operation of the missiles from reaching Cuba. The blockade bought Kennedy and his advisers time. If Khrushchev refused to withdraw the missiles, then Kennedy could authorise the bombing of the missile sites or a full-scale invasion of Cuba.

Kennedy then went on national television to explain the American position to the public. He called the blockade a 'quarantine', since technically a naval blockade was an act of war. Ships approaching Cuba would be searched and those carrying military equipment would be asked to return to their port of origin. Khrushchev ignored the quarantine and instructed Soviet forces on Cuba to adopt a state of full alert. He also denied the presence of missile sites on the island. Two very tense days followed. Soviet ships escorted by a submarine were rapidly approaching the quarantine line around Cuba. The US aircraft carrier *Essex* was ordered to signal the Soviet submarine to surface. If the submarine refused to comply, depth charges were to be used. Many policy-makers now expected war. Kennedy confided in his brother, 'It looks really mean, doesn't it?' At this point the President received news that six Russian vessels had either stopped or turned back for the Soviet Union. The relief in Washington was almost tangible. Secretary of State Rusk turned to National Security Adviser Bundy and commented, 'We're eyeball to eyeball and I think the other fellow just blinked.' For the moment war had been averted, but the Russians had said nothing about the missile sites on Cuba. The crisis continued.

At the outset of the crisis Kennedy had wanted an unconditional withdrawal of Soviet missiles from Cuba. After 25 October, however, he realised that the United States might have to offer some concessions to secure the evacuation of the missiles. A fallback position was even prepared in case the Russians did not remove the missiles: the United States would ask the United Nations Secretary-General U Thant to place Soviet missile installations in Cuba and US sites in Turkey under United Nations supervision. The secret discussion of the referral of the issue to the United Nations suggests that perhaps Kennedy would not in the end have used military force to remove the missiles and that the threat of air strikes and an invasion was merely a bluff. We shall never know the answer. However, the existence of such a contingency plan shows how keen Kennedy was to avoid war with the Soviet Union over the issue of missiles on Cuba.

Kennedy's willingness to compromise was tested by a telegram from Khrushchev on 26 October. The Soviet leader offered to dismantle the missiles in return for an undertaking by the United States not to invade Cuba. The Americans did not respond immediately. Initially Kennedy was unwilling to give such a pledge. Many members of Congress and the public supported the overthrow of Castro by an invasion. A commitment not to invade Cuba would have restricted America's policy options in the future. While ExComm was considering how to respond to Khrushchev's first telegram, the Soviet leader sent a second message offering different terms for the removal of the missiles. He now attached two conditions to the withdrawal of the missiles: a non-invasion pledge and the removal of American Jupiter missiles from Turkey. The difference between the first and second messages has puzzled historians. When the Russians sent the first message, they thought that an American invasion of Cuba was imminent. Khrushchev was as determined as Kennedy to avoid a war and asked for the non-invasion pledge as the best concession the Soviet Union was likely to get in return for removing the missiles. However, by the time of the second message Soviet intelligence had reported that an immediate invasion was unlikely. Khrushchev therefore decided to attempt to strike a better bargain and attach new conditions to the removal of the missiles.

The crisis now intensified. Many members of ExComm opposed trading the Jupiters for Soviet missiles on Cuba. At any moment the confrontation could have escalated into open war. B-52 bombers circled Cuba in preparation for an air strike. There was a massive military build-up within the United States. Forces gathered in Florida ready for an invasion. On 26 October a surface-to-air missile brought down a U-2 over Cuba killing the pilot. Some of Kennedy's advisers saw this as the first shot and called for an assault on Cuba. The pressure for military action within policy-making circles was building. On the following day a U-2 strayed into Soviet airspace. The Russians protested but took no action. Unknown to the Americans at the time, 20 nuclear warheads were already on Cuba and 42 of the IRBMs were operational. Castro expected war. He spent the night of 26 October in a bomb shelter in Havana. The second week of the missile crisis was more fraught with danger than the first.

The President himself saw military action as a last resort. He recognised that Soviet insistence on dismantling the Jupiters was not unreasonable. He conceded as much in an exchange with his National Security Adviser, McGeorge Bundy, during an ExComm meeting. He was clearly thinking in terms of a compromise.

1 *Kennedy:* He's [Khrushchev] got us in a pretty good spot here, because most people will regard this as not an unreasonable proposal, I'll just tell you that. In fact, in many ways -
Bundy [disagreeing with Kennedy]: But what most people, Mr.
5 President?
Kennedy: I think you're going to find it very difficult to explain why we are going to take hostile military action in Cuba against those sites - what we've been thinking about - the thing that he's saying is, 'If you'll get yours out of Turkey, we'll get ours out of Cuba.' I
10 think we've got a very tough one here.

On his brother's advice he now ignored Khrushchev's first message and responded to the second. The United States formally offered a commitment not to invade Cuba in return for the removal of the missiles. At the same time the President sent his brother to see Anatoly Dobrynin, the Soviet ambassador in Washington, in order to assure him that the Jupiters would be taken out of Turkey. Robert Kennedy remembered telling Dobrynin the following.

1 We had to have a commitment by tomorrow that the bases would be removed. I was not giving them an ultimatum but a statement of fact. He should understand that if they did not remove those bases, we would remove them. He asked me about what offer the United
5 States was making and I told him of the letter that President Kennedy had just transmitted to Khrushchev. He raised the question of our removing the missiles from Turkey. I said that there could be no quid pro quo or any arrangement made under this kind of threat or pressure. However, I said, President Kennedy
10 had been anxious to remove those missiles from Turkey for a long period of time. He had ordered their removal some time ago and it was our judgement that, within a short time after the crisis was over, those missiles would be gone. Time was running out. We had only a few more hours - we needed an answer immediately from
20 the Soviet Union. I said we must have it the next day.

The day after Robert Kennedy's session with Dobrynin, Khrushchev cabled Washington. Armed with a guarantee about the removal of the Jupiters from Turkey, he promised to take the Soviet missiles off Cuba in exchange for the undertaking the Americans had given not to invade the island. The Soviet leader was as relieved as Kennedy to extricate himself from the crisis without losing face and without going to war. There was no explicit reference to the Jupiters in Khrushchev's cable. Kennedy was adamant that this aspect of the deal should remain secret. Openly to trade the Jupiters for the Soviet missiles on Cuba would have made him look weak. The Jupiters were withdrawn in April 1963, but the American public were not told for six years. News of Robert Kennedy's secret diplomacy did not emerge for 25 years. In November U-2 reconnaissance photographs showed workers bulldozing the missile sites and loading military equipment onto ships to be returned to the Soviet Union. The missile crisis was over.

c) Consequences

Kennedy gained politically and personally from the missile crisis. The Democrats retained control of both houses of Congress following the mid-term elections in November 1962. The President's own stature also grew. The outcome of the crisis was seen as a personal triumph: he had achieved the evacuation of the missiles from Cuba and avoided a nuclear war with the Soviet Union. His management of the crisis compensated for the Bay of Pigs fiasco and the unproductive Vienna summit. The voters were unaware that the resolution of the crisis had been only a partial victory achieved at a high price. As a quid pro quo for the removal of the missiles he had given an undertaking in public not to invade Cuba and a commitment in private to dismantle the Jupiters in Turkey. His initial hopes of an unconditional Soviet withdrawal of the missiles had been vain. Khrushchev's gambit of installing missiles on Cuba had forced Kennedy into concessions he would not otherwise have made.

The most obvious effects of the missile crisis occurred in the sphere of US-Soviet relations. Both Kennedy and Khrushchev had been sobered by the experience of being on the brink of nuclear war and now initiated a period of detente. A 'hot line' between Moscow and Washington was set up. A link between the two capitals allowed secure and rapid communication at the highest level in an emergency and reduced the possibility of accidental war. Both superpowers also supported a UN resolution prohibiting the deployment of weapons in outer space. The Americans agreed to sell $250 million of surplus grain to the Russians. The most significant breakthrough, however, was the Test Ban Treaty agreed in June 1963. The United States, the Soviet Union and Britain each agreed to cease atmospheric testing of nuclear weapons (underground testing was permitted). One of Kennedy's last major speeches on foreign affairs captured the new spirit of co-operation between Moscow and Washington.

1 History teaches us that enmities between nations do not last forever. Among the many traits the peoples of our two countries have in common, none is stronger than our mutual abhorrence of war. Almost unique among the major world powers, we have never 5 been at war with each other. If we cannot now end our differences, at least we can help make the world safe for diversity. For in the final analysis our most basic common link is the fact that we all inhabit this planet. We all breathe the same air. We all cherish our children's future. And we are all mortal.

Relations between Cuba and the United States remained largely unaffected by the missile crisis. Kennedy briefly explored the possibility of negotiations with Castro via unofficial contacts. But in June 1963 he ordered the resumption of Operation Mongoose. Acts of economic sabotage on Cuba, piracy against Cuban vessels and isolated coastal raids were orchestrated by the CIA. Plans to assassinate Castro also remained in place. What the Americans could no longer achieve by invasion they attempted to achieve by covert action.

6 Kennedy and the Cold War: An Assessment

Kennedy's handling of the Cold War was marked by both successes and failures. In the summer of 1961 he skilfully conducted a war of nerves with Khrushchev. Eisenhower's first summit occurred three years into his presidency, whereas Kennedy had to negotiate with Khrushchev after only six months in the White House. He gave no ground to the Russians at the Vienna summit and subsequently showed Khrushchev that Soviet pressure would not extract concessions from the United

States. The safeguarding of the West's position in Berlin was a considerable achievement. The Cuban missile crisis perhaps showed Kennedy at his best. His policies may have been partly responsible for the deployment of Soviet missiles on Cuba in the first place, and the resolution of the crisis was achieved at a higher price than the American public knew. Nevertheless, his skill in crisis management was considerable. He resisted pressure from within his administration for the early use of military force and sought every available means of removing the missiles short of going to war with the Soviet Union. In testing circumstances Kennedy demonstrated a cool head, a capacity for clear thinking, and an instinct for compromise which belied his public persona of toughness. The missile crisis also revealed the merits of the strategy of flexible response. Confronted by Soviet missiles on Cuba, Kennedy had more cards to play than simply threatening the Russians with massive retaliation. Preventive measures such as the quarantine, the threat of military action and negotiation all contributed to the ending of the crisis. At the time of Kennedy's death US-Soviet relations were better than at any previous moment in the Cold War. The 'hot line' and the Test Ban Treaty represented the true beginnings of detente, while on the broader strategic front Kennedy's investment in more missiles ensured that America maintained nuclear superiority at least in the short term. The price of strategic superiority was an escalating arms race with the Soviet Union and budget deficits at home.

Kennedy also recorded some notable failures. The aims of the Alliance for Progress were noble, but the actual aid to Latin American countries never approached the $20 billion promised. The aid that was sent was spent on arms and not on tackling the structural economic problems of Latin America which made the countries in the region vulnerable to communism. In 1963 even Kennedy was privately pessimistic about the Alliance. Perhaps Kennedy's worst single error was to authorise the Bay of Pigs invasion. The bungled operation frightened Castro, drove Cuba closer to Moscow and offered Khrushchev a pretext for positioning missiles on the island the following year. The cease-fire in Laos prevented a potential confrontation between the superpowers in south-east Asia, but it did little to counter communism there. Instability in Laos and the continued progress of the Pathet Lao only made it harder to defend adjacent South Vietnam against communist infiltration.

Although Vietnam was never considered a high priority by Kennedy, his administration's biggest policy failure probably occurred there. The scale of the problem confronting Kennedy was greater than under Eisenhower because of the rapid growth of communist incursion in 1961, but Kennedy was no more successful than Ike in extinguishing communism in South Vietnam. American backing for a corrupt and unpopular leader and indiscriminate counter-insurgency operations in the Vietnamese countryside only increased support for the Vietcong and compounded the very problem the Americans were trying to solve. In private Kennedy and his advisers appreciated that not all communist forces were answerable to Moscow and Beijing. Yet in practice Kennedy's actions in Vietnam were based on the flawed premise that international communism was a monolith. Policy-makers wrongly assumed that the Vietcong were being directed by China and the Soviet Union. Vietnam therefore assumed a strategic importance it did not warrant and Kennedy sent ever more military advisers and ever more aid. We can never know whether Kennedy would have committed the United States to war in Vietnam, but it remains true that the Americans were more entangled in Vietnam in 1963 than they had been in 1961.

To sum up, Kennedy's record in handling the Cold War was mixed. Following his assassination in 1963 his political reputation was high. Americans then rated him as one of their best presidents. Historians since have been more critical. It is up to the reader to decide whether he was a great Cold War leader or an adequate president who may have grown into a statesman of real stature had he lived longer.

Making notes on 'Crisis and Compromise: Kennedy's Cold War, 1961-3'

Use the chapter headings and the end-of-chapter summary diagram as the skeleton of your notes. Approach this chapter with questions in mind and organise your notes around answers to those questions. What were the main elements of Kennedy's policy of containment? What were the similarities and differences between Eisenhower's and Kennedy's policies of containment? You should then consider Indochina as a test case of the strategy of 'flexible response'. What were the goals and methods of US policy in Laos and to what extent was US policy there successful? Your notes on Vietnam should be more detailed. Why did Kennedy and his advisers attach such importance to Vietnam? How did the US respond to the communist infiltration of South Vietnam? Identify reasons for the failure of the policy of containment in South Vietnam. Then you should turn your attention to the personal confrontation between Kennedy and Khrushchev in this period. How did the US react to Soviet attempts to push the Western powers out of Berlin? How well did Kennedy deal with Khrushchev during the Berlin crisis of 1961? When making notes on the Cuban Missile Crisis, you might want to divide your notes into the causes, course and consequences of the crisis. You could cover the story of the crisis briefly. A simple timeline will suffice. But you should pay attention to the causes and effects of the crisis. In the final section of your notes you should be weighing up Kennedy's record as a Cold War leader, listing what you think were his strengths and weaknesses and measuring his achievements against his goals.

Answering essay questions on *'Crisis and Compromise: Kennedy's Cold War, 1961 3'*

Essay questions on the Cold War under Kennedy are most likely to be similar to the following:

1   Contrast Eisenhower's and Kennedy's policies of containment.
2   Why did the United States find it so difficult to halt the advance of communism in South Vietnam under Kennedy?
3   Why did the Cuban missile crisis not end in war between the United States and the Soviet Union?

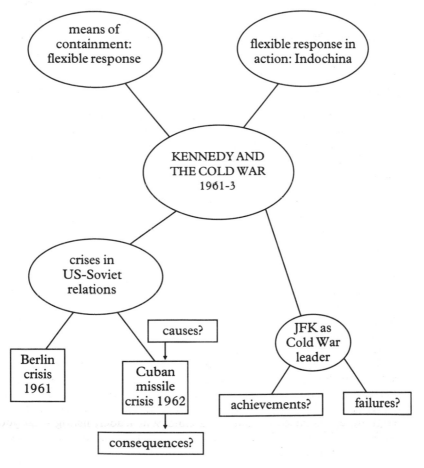

Summary - Crisis and Compromise: Kennedy's Cold War, 1961-3

4   'An unqualified triumph.' Evaluate this verdict on Kennedy's management of the Cuban missile crisis.
5   To what extent was the Cuban missile crisis a turning point in US policy in the Cold War?

In question 1 the key instruction word is 'contrast'. 'Contrast' prompts you to consider two things in relation to each other, highlighting differences between the two. But you should also show an awareness of similarities. It might be sensible to contrast Eisenhower's and Kennedy's policies of containment under two headings, aims and methods. Make a list of differences between the 'New Look' and 'flexible response' under these headings. A good essay might also explain why those differences existed. In the second part of your essay you might show that you are also aware of similarities between the 'New Look' and 'flexible response'. Detail similarities in aims and methods between the two policies of containment.

The remaining four questions all fall into categories already discussed in some detail in previous 'Answering Essay Questions' sections. Build your response to question 2 around the reasons for the failure of containment in South Vietnam. Do not fall into the narrative trap, simply describing what happened in South Vietnam. Aim for linkage. Try to make the connection between the point you are discussing and the American failure to defeat communism in South Vietnam. For question 3 you have to explain the peaceful resolution of the Cuban missile crisis. The attitudes of the protagonists are important. Both Kennedy and Khrushchev did not want war. You might place Kennedy's and Khrushchev's views in a broader context, pointing out that both men realised that full-scale war between the United States and the Soviet Union would result in extensive destruction on both sides. You need to examine diplomacy during the crisis in some detail and explain how both leaders were able to extricate themselves from the crisis without losing face. Consequently, they did not have to resort to force.

In question 4 you will have to decide how well the statement in inverted commas fits Kennedy's conduct of the crisis. Your response will need to be balanced. In some respects the outcome of the crisis was a victory for Kennedy. On the other hand, it was not a total victory. What evidence can you find to support each side of the argument? What will be your overall verdict? Question 5 is asking you to think about continuity and change in US policy before and after the Cuban missile crisis. Think of examples of changes in US policy attributable directly to the crisis. Here you might consider the thaw in US-Soviet relations in the aftermath of the crisis. On the other hand, some aspects of US policy did not change, for example US policy towards Cuba. The relative extent of continuity and change will shape your view on whether or not the Cuban Missile Crisis was a turning point.

Source-based questions on 'Crisis and Compromise: Kennedy's Cold War, 1961-3'

1 US Policy in Vietnam under Kennedy
Read the extract on page 112 and answer the following questions.
a) What reservations does Kennedy express about the way Diem was governing South Vietnam? (2 marks)
b) What conclusions can you draw from this source about how the United States was attempting to contain communism in South Vietnam? (4 marks)
c) Why might a historian be cautious about accepting statements made by Kennedy in a television interview as reliable evidence about the course of US policy in Vietnam? (4 marks)

2 Robert Kennedy's Meeting with Soviet Ambassador Dobrynin, October 1962
Read the extract on page 121 and answer the following questions.
a) In the context of the extract, explain the term 'bases' (line 1). (1 mark)
b) How useful is this extract to a historian inquiring into US diplomacy during the missile crisis? (4 marks)
c) Does this extract satisfactorily explain why the Cuban missile crisis did not erupt into open war between the United States and the Soviet Union? (5 marks)

CHAPTER 7

Home Front: The Impact of the Cold War on the United States, 1945–63

1 Politics: The Cold War Presidency

The onset of the Cold War and America's arrival as a superpower transformed the institution of the presidency. Successive presidents spent much of their time engaged in foreign policy and steadily expanded the powers of the president in foreign policy making. The limits imposed on presidential freedom of action by the constitution were pushed back and presidents exercised ever greater control over foreign policy at the expense of Congress. In particular the war- and treaty-making powers of the presidency grew.

In June 1950 Truman sent troops to Korea without Congressional authorisation. This was a clear infringement of Congress's right to declare war on behalf of the United States. Both Truman and his Secretary of State justified the action in several ways. Since American troops were being despatched as part of a United Nations force, Truman likened intervention in Korea to a 'police action' and not a war. His Secretary of State, Dean Acheson, argued that an immediate response to the invasion of South Korea by the North was required. A Congressional declaration of war would only have created delay and hamstrung America's attempt to cope with the emergency in Korea. Military aggression by communist North Korea had produced an atmosphere of crisis. Against this background Truman could cite the paramount importance of the containment of communism as grounds for deploying American forces immediately without prior authority from Congress. The Senate endorsed Truman's actions several days later by voting funds for the war and introducing selective service, but in fact Truman had unilaterally taken the United States into a major war. Truman faced little opposition in the Senate, although there were one or two dissenting voices. Senator Robert Taft complained that the President could now 'send troops to Tibet ... or to Indo-China or anywhere else in the world without the slightest voice of Congress in the matter'. Senator Arthur Watkins accurately described the situation when he stated that the 'United States is at war by order of the President.' Truman's conduct in 1950 enlarged the power of future presidents to take the United States into major wars, and during the conflict in Vietnam presidents exploited these new-found powers until Congress reasserted its historic war powers under the War Powers Act in 1973.

There was a similar erosion of the treaty-making powers of Congress in the post-war period. Increasingly pacts with other countries took the form of executive agreements which were concluded by the president alone. In our period US nuclear bases were established in Spain and Morocco by executive agreement. Since such agreements were not formal treaties they were not subject to approval by a two-thirds majority in the Senate. The Senate attempted to reassert its traditional rights in this area when Senator Bricker introduced an amendment which invalidated any international agreements made by the president unless they were approved by Congress, but the Bricker Amendment was defeated twice in 1952 and 1954.

Three other developments altered the balance of power between president and Congress in the field of foreign policy. Firstly, the maintenance of a large peacetime army during the Cold War meant that a president's powers as commander-in-chief were now much wider. He could deploy American forces around the globe without reference to Congress. In 1948, for example, Truman independently ordered American forces to mount the Berlin Airlift. In 1951 at the height of the Korean War, he sent US troops to Germany to reinforce NATO, again without consulting Congress. This was another decision ratified by Congress after the fact. Secondly, the invention of nuclear weapons had changed the conventions of war-making. A major conflict need not now be preceded by a formal declaration of war but might be triggered by a surprise nuclear strike by the Soviet Union. In those circumstances a president might have to make an instant decision on the use of nuclear weapons for the sake of national survival. There would not be time to convene Congress. The 1787 constitution's provisions on war powers had been overtaken by technology. Finally, the creation of the CIA served to exclude Congress from important decisions about foreign policy. The Central Intelligence Act in 1949 had conceded wide-ranging powers to the CIA and meant that it was effectively unaccountable to Congress. The result was that some secret operations were mounted jointly by the White House and the CIA beyond the scrutiny of the legislature. In 1961 the Bay of Pigs invasion was planned and executed by the CIA without the knowledge of Congress.

The increased powers of the executive in foreign policy in the early Cold War period have led some historians to see the emergence of an 'imperial presidency'. Worldwide interests made post-war America an imperial power and as leaders of an imperial power presidents wielded huge authority. The constitutional restraints on the powers of the executive were violated as successive presidents limited the role of the legislature in foreign policy and used the authority inherent in their position to the full to deploy American forces across the world, make war and strike agreements with foreign states.

2 Society

a) The 'Red Scare'

Heightened fears about communism abroad were accompanied by a new anxiety about communism at home. From 1947 until the mid-1950s America was in the grip of a 'Red Scare'. There was an almost paranoid belief that America's major institutions had been infiltrated by communists or communist sympathisers. Fifth columnists were seen everywhere, pro-Soviet enemies within intent on bringing down the American government and way of life. What followed was a concerted attempt to eliminate communists from every sphere of American life.

The federal government targeted suspected communists within its own ranks with the introduction of loyalty tests for employees in 1947. Links with any communist organisation constituted disloyalty and provided grounds for dismissal. If recommended for dismissal, employees had a right to appeal to the Loyalty Review Board. These boards often cross-examined federal jobholders about their political views. One employee was asked if he owned any books about the government of Russia, another if he possessed any records of music by Russian composers.

The Eightieth Congress elected in 1946 typified the anti-communist spirit of the age. The House Committee on Un-American Activities (HUAC) played a leading role in investigating communist activity. In 1947 it turned its attention to Hollywood. The American Right had long suspected that the motion picture industry was home to many radicals, something it thought was important as it recognised the potential of cinema as a medium for influencing the opinions of the masses. In fact, the small American Communist Party (CPUSA) had 300 members in Hollywood, many of them screenwriters. In 1947 leading figures in the film industry were summoned to hearings by the HUAC. Some were or had been party members but refused to discuss their political beliefs. They became known as the Hollywood Ten. At first Hollywood stood by the Ten and a Committee for the First Amendment (the First Amendment of the US Constitution guaranteed free speech) was formed, which included stars like Humphrey Bogart, Lauren Bacall and Katherine Hepburn. However, support for the Ten quickly crumbled in response to public opinion. In two towns boycotts of films starring supporters of the Ten occurred and one audience stoned a screen on which a Katherine Hepburn film was being shown. Hollywood producers and directors, nervous of losing their audience, promptly withdrew support from the Ten. The film actors' union, the Screen Actors Guild, operated a blacklist of suspected communists who were not employed by the studios. Its president from 1947 to 1952 was Ronald Reagan, later to become president of the United States. Reagan helped the Federal Bureau of Investigation (FBI) identify actors who were sympathetic to communist ideas. Anti-communists in Hollywood formed the Motion Picture Alliance for the Preservation of American Ideals, dedicated to making patriotic films. Its early members included John Wayne and Walt Disney.

The search for communists extended to schools and universities. Loyalty oaths were required from teachers. The classroom must not be used as a forum for feeding communist propaganda to gullible young minds. Right-wingers warned of the 'the little Red schoolhouse'. The magazine of the patriotic organisation, the American Legion, carried alarmist articles such as 'Your Child is Their Target'. Textbooks as well as teachers came under suspicion. In 1949 the HUAC asked for reading lists from over seventy universities and colleges. University lecturers were subjected to close scrutiny. American campuses were seen as nurseries of left-wing ideas. Anti-communists believed that the lecture-room should be the 'chapel of democracy'. In 1948 three professors at the University of Washington were fired for alleged links with the CPUSA. They never found another academic post. At the University of California 31 academics were dismissed.

Another sanctuary for communists had been the American labour movement. But by the late 1940s the Congress of Industrial Organisations (CIO), an American equivalent of the TUC in Britain, launched a campaign against its communist members. At their 1949 convention, the CIO expelled the pro-communist Farm Equipment Workers and United Electrical Workers. Nine more communist-led unions were later expelled from the movement.

Unsurprisingly, the CPUSA itself fell victim to the 'Red Scare'. In 1948 the Truman administration prosecuted leading figures within the party. The outbreak of the Korean War two years later and the prevailing hostility to communism made some sort of anti-communist legislation a certainty. The outcome was the Internal Security Act of 1950, also known as the McCarran Act because it was introduced by the Democrat Senator for Nevada, Patrick McCarran. It required all communists to identify themselves and register with the Justice Department, denied federal government jobs and US passports to party members and outlawed them from working in defence plants.

b) McCarthyism

Senator Joseph McCarthy of Wisconsin rode the crest of the anti-communist wave. In February 1950 he claimed that he had a list of 205 employees in the State Department who were members of the Communist Party. He said that although their names had been passed to the Secretary of State, they remained in employment. In the face of questioning by reporters, he later changed the figure to 57. This was to become a common pattern. McCarthy would brand individuals as communists without producing any hard evidence and would then frequently change his story. He was the supreme 'Red-baiter'. He gave his name to the period - the early 1950s are often known as the 'McCarthy era' - and the relentless search for communists in American public life became known as McCarthyism.

McCarthy's initial allegations in 1950 were designed to rescue his own political career. Elected in 1946, his record in the Senate was undistinguished and he was looking for a way to make his name before facing the voters again in 1952. In this sense he was successful: his campaign against communists at home clinched his re-election as senator in 1952. McCarthy's motives, however, were more than party political. He had his own agenda and his 'Red-baiting' was an expression of continuing regional, religious and class divisions in American society. McCarthy, like those who voted for him, was from the mid-west, Roman Catholic, and from an ordinary social background. Many of those whom he labelled as communists or communist sympathisers were from the east coast, protestant and members of the upper class, having attended private schools and prestigious universities. Truman's Secretary of State, Dean Acheson, fitted the mould perfectly. He personified the privileged, liberal east coast Establishment and was loathed by the McCarthyites. McCarthy's denigration of such men was at one level an expression of smouldering class resentment and fierce regional and religious loyalties.

McCarthy scattered accusations of communism widely, but initially he concentrated his fire on members of the State Department. He saw State as a haven for liberals and left-wingers who were tolerant of communist ideas. Consequently, he believed, the State Department had not given Jiang enough support in the Chinese civil war and was responsible for the 'loss' of China. McCarthy's allegations may have been inaccurate and exaggerated but the fact that he enjoyed the support of leading Republicans bolstered his stature. The times also lent credibility to McCarthy. China had just been taken over by communists, the Russians had an A-bomb, and a German-born physicist, Klaus Fuchs, who had worked on the Manhattan Project, had just been convicted of espionage in Britain for having leaked atomic secrets to the Russians. The outbreak of the Korean War provided the perfect backdrop for him. All these events had fuelled public concern about communism and generated a 'Red scare.' McCarthy now played on those fears by uncovering the communist enemy within.

McCarthy's hunt for communists intensified after his return to the Senate in 1952. He used the Permanent Subcommittee on Investigations, a part of the obscure Government Operations Committee, as his platform. He resumed his attack on the State Department, forcing the removal of all unpatriotic and left-wing books from State Department libraries overseas. In 1953 McCarthy was at the peak of his influence, but he now overreached himself. His committee challenged the patriotism of the American armed forces by undertaking an investigation into communism in the US Army. The committee's hearings were a turning point. Firstly, McCarthy found very little evidence of communist sympathies within the Army. Secondly, the Army-McCarthy hearings were televised from April to June 1954 and watched by a daytime audience of as many as 20 million. The American public did not like what they saw. McCarthy was a heavy drinker and sometimes slept in his office in the Senate. He appeared unshaven and rumpled and looked sinister on television. Moreover, his treatment of witnesses was heavy-handed. He shouted at them and interrupted them. Opinion polls in June indicated a shift in public attitudes towards McCarthy. Previously 50 per cent of respondents had supported him. The figure was now 34 per cent, while the proportion of people with a negative opinion of him increased from 29 per cent to 45 per cent. McCarthy's colleagues in the Senate now turned against him and a vote of censure was passed against him by 67 votes to 22. He was censured not for his anti-communist views but for his conduct. He had described one liberal Republican colleague as 'senile - I think they should get a man with a net and take him to a good quiet place'. Another was 'a living miracle in that he is without question the only man who has lived for so long with neither brains nor guts'. Such reckless attacks were seen as breaches of the Senate's etiquette and McCarthy even lost the support of his own party. Twenty-two of those who had voted in favour of censure were Republicans. McCarthy was now a spent force and with his downfall the 'Red Scare' receded but did not disappear. He died of a liver condition in 1957 while still a United States Senator.

c) Causes of the Red Scare

The origins of the 'Red Scare' were complex. Some of the major institutions of American society in the 1940s undoubtedly fostered a mood of anti-communism. The press was a powerful opinion-former. News magazines such as *Time* and *Newsweek* were vociferously anti-communist, as was the mass circulation magazine *Reader's Digest*. The nation's two most influential newspapers, the *New York Times* and the *Washington Post*, were fierce critics of the regimes in Beijing and Moscow and their columnists frequently argued that America was losing the Cold War. The largest national newspaper chain, owned by the Hearst family, shared their hostility. The church too played a role. The Roman Catholic Church was an enthusiastic participant in 'Red-hunting'. The atheism of the Soviet regime and the persecution of Catholics behind the Iron Curtain had anyway created a strong bias against communism among Catholic clergy. The pulpit was an effective platform for expressing disapproval of communism. Cardinal Spellman was a prominent supporter of McCarthy and fed the FBI with information on suspected communists. In 1946 he stated his position clearly:

A true American can be neither a communist nor a Communist condoner and we realise that the first loyalty of every American is vigilantly to weed out and counteract Communism and convert every American Communist to Americanism.

Evangelical preachers also shaped the thinking of their followers in fiercely anti-communist sermons. The evangelist Billy Graham, assisted by regular exposure in Hearst-owned papers, established his reputation in this period. At mass prayer meetings in California, where people would come forward and declare themselves for God, he would preach on the evils of communism. The following extract is typical:

1 Do you know that the Fifth Columnists, called Communists, are
  more rampant in Los Angeles than any other city in America? ...
  The world is divided into two camps! On the one side we see
  Communism has declared war against God, against Christ, against
5 the Bible, and against all religion ...

It was a familiar message. On the one hand the United States was identified with God and good, on the other communism was linked to the Devil, sin and evil. The words 'under God' were added by Congress to the Pledge of Allegiance which was recited daily by American schoolchildren in the presence of the national flag. Congress wanted to make the point that the United States was a godly nation, whereas the Marxist Soviet Union condoned atheism. The capacity of American churches to influence the views of their believers should not be underestimated, particularly at a time of increasing church attendance. Church membership increased from 49 per cent of the population in 1940 to 69 per cent in 1960.

There had been a strong undercurrent of anti-communism in America since 1917. The 'Red Scare' in 1919-20 (see page 13) was only one example. The HUAC had in fact been established before the war in 1938 to investigate not only suspected American Nazis but communists too. But in the 1940s and 1950s the latent hostility to communism rose to the surface and assumed new forms. Events brought the fear of communism into sharper focus. The fact that by 1947 America's principal external enemy was a communist state intensified opposition to communism at home. Events in 1949 and 1950 also lent momentum to the 'Red Scare'. The explosion of the Soviet atomic bomb made Russia seem a more dangerous enemy and seemed to lend substance to the theory that spies were passing America's atomic secrets to the other side. Many Americans thought that any communist state must be technologically backward. How could Russia have acquired the bomb other than by spying on the West? The 'fall' of China marked another victory for communism. The outbreak of the Korean War clarified the issue further. American troops were fighting against communist North

Korean and Chinese armies. It followed that American communists were therefore disloyal and unpatriotic. Their allegiance lay with the enemy. The actions of the Truman administration were also partly responsible for the 'Red Scare'. In 1947 Truman had followed Acheson's advice to frighten Congress into voting financial aid to Greece and Turkey by knowingly exaggerating the menace of communism. The overstatement of the communist threat abroad heightened popular fears about communists at home and sowed the seeds for McCarthyism. Truman had created a climate of opinion in which McCarthy's allegations seemed credible.

Opportunist politicians also pandered to popular anxieties about communism. Republicans sought to discredit opponents and advance their own careers by labelling Democrats as 'communists' or 'soft on communism'. They soon discovered that the tactic paid dividends at the polls. The future President, Richard Nixon, captured a Congressional seat in southern California in 1946 after repeatedly associating his opponent, Jerry Voorhis, with communists. Nixon used the same methods four years later against his Democrat opponent, Helen Gahagan Douglas, in a successful campaign for the Senate. His supporters circulated 'pink sheets' detailing Douglas's leftist votes as a Senator. The whole issue of communism at home became entangled in party politics. Democrats had occupied the White House since 1932 and Republicans were searching for a vote-winning issue. As early as 1944 the Republican presidential candidate, Thomas Dewey, had denounced Franklin Roosevelt as a communist on account of his New Deal policies which had seen an unprecedented degree of government intervention in the lives of Americans. Truman's unexpected victory in the 1948 presidential election was a major setback for the Republicans and they attempted to recover support by consistently smearing Democrats as communists or communist sympathisers.

d) Consequences of the 'Red Scare'

The 'Red Scare' was irrational in that it targeted an enemy which did not really exist. In the mid-1950s membership of the CPUSA stood at only 5,000 many of whom were FBI infiltrators. Communism had never commanded much support in the United States. A survey at the height of the 'Red Scare' in 1954 found that only 10 per cent of Americans had known people they even suspected of being a communist. McCarthy also lacked mass public support. Only once, at the beginning of 1954, did more than 50 per cent of Americans say that they backed him.

Yet the consequences of the 'Red Scare' were profound and diverse. One important outcome was the erosion of civil liberties. New parameters were imposed on freedom of thought and expression, as federal employees found themselves summoned before Loyalty Boards or schoolteachers were called before School Boards to explain their views.

Under Eisenhower loyalty tests became even more stringent. Workers in all federal departments or agencies could be summarily dismissed if 'reasonable doubt' existed about their suitability for government employment. Under Eisenhower the State Department was purged of suspected communists. Communist sympathisers who were resident in the United States but not US citizens were expelled and alleged communists seeking entry to the United States were barred. Civil liberties were also threatened by the Federal Bureau of Investigation (FBI), a government agency responsible for internal security. The head of the FBI was J. Edgar Hoover, an obsessive anti-communist, and his agency was an important arm of the campaign against communism. The FBI kept extensive records on suspected radicals, placed left-wingers under surveillance, and tapped their telephones. In 1954 the 'the father of the atomic bomb', J. Robert Oppenheimer, was deemed a security risk on account of left-wing friends and relatives. This followed six months of investigation by the FBI during which Oppenheimer's home had been bugged and his telephone tapped.

Some Americans were aware of the danger posed to the American way of life by the campaign against communists at home. Truman himself appreciated that safeguards against communism could at the same time act as checks on essential American freedoms. He vetoed the Internal Security Act in 1950 on the grounds that it contravened the right to free speech, but the veto was overturned by Congress. He also harboured doubts about the activities of the FBI, privately noting that 'We want no Gestapo or Secret Police. FBI is tending in that direction.' A common complaint against communist states was that they silenced opposition parties, employed secret police forces and prohibited free speech. Yet the federal government's actions against the CPUSA, their surveillance of communist suspects, and their introduction of loyalty tests were not so very different. The United States was in danger of destroying at home the very freedoms it was waging the Cold War abroad in order to protect.

An atmosphere of fear was another legacy of the McCarthy era. People thought twice before expressing a point of view which might be misinterpreted and reported to the FBI. In 1947 the singer and actor Frank Sinatra had voiced the fear that 'If you make a pitch on a nationwide radio network for a square deal for the underdog, will they call you a Commie?' It was this sort of feeling that prevented many in the mainstream of American political life from exposing McCarthy's allegations for the lies they were. People were simply too frightened. McCarthy operated in a world of black and white. To attack McCarthy was to defend communism and a priori to reveal oneself as a communist and so substantiate his original allegations. Across America librarians put left-wing books into storage in order to avoid the finger of suspicion. In the late 1950s one-third of librarians reported having removed 'controversial' items from their shelves, such as works by Marx. After the

HUAC investigations of 1947, American film directors stopped making films with a message. Any film which addressed social issues like race or poverty might be interpreted as over-sympathetic to the working man and left-wing and place the director on a blacklist. For most Americans the 1950s were a good decade, a period of increasing living standards and rising expectations. But the internal divisions, as Americans turned on one another, and the fears generated by McCarthy cast a lengthy shadow across the optimism and affluence of the early 1950s.

The 'Red Scare' also solidified existing anti-communist sentiment. A poll in 1947 revealed that 61 per cent of respondents favoured outlawing the Communist Party. Anti-communism was firmly planted in the American consciousness and at local level expressions of anti-communist feeling were often intense. In 1953 Ethel and Julius Rosenberg were sentenced to death for membership of a spy ring which had passed atomic secrets to the Russians. A campaign was mounted against the death sentence but it fell on deaf ears. As the date of their execution approached, demonstrators appeared outside the White House with signs reading 'FRY 'EM WELL DONE.' When Nikita Khrushchev visited the United States in 1959, one protester greeted him with the sign, 'The only good communist is a dead communist.' A narrower definition of who was American now prevailed. Professing communist beliefs and being an American were incompatible in the eyes of most. 'Communist' became a term of abuse applied by one person or group to others whose views they disagreed with. Hence opponents of homosexuality dubbed gay men as communists; segregationists in the South described supporters of civil rights as communists.

Anti-communism was not only a dominant strain in public opinion, it united America's governing class. A consensus existed within both parties that the central thrust of American foreign policy should be anti-communist. Left-wing Democrats and right-wing Republicans consistently voted substantial funds to the Defence Department and shared the view that the Soviet Union was the enemy. The policy of containing communism was unquestioned in this period. Anti-communism was so deeply rooted that not one Senator publicly supported a change in policy towards Russia or the recognition of mainland China between 1953 and 1962.

Many forms of popular culture mirrored the prevailing anti-communist mood. As ever, Hollywood was a good barometer of popular attitudes. Wartime films had portrayed the Soviet Union in a rosy light. In *The North Star* (1943) peasants on a Soviet collective farm heroically resisted German invaders. Now, however, Russians received less favourable treatment and some films were little more than crude anti-communist propaganda. *My Son John* (1952) was a classic example of the genre. John is his mother's favourite son, but while his two brothers enlist to fight in Korea, he works as a spy for the Russians in Washington. Discovered by his mother, he is turned over to the FBI. He sees the error of his ways and prepares a speech disowning communism, but is assassinated by party comrades on the steps of the Lincoln Memorial in Washington for betraying the party. His speech is then delivered posthumously in front of freshman students at his former university:

> Even now the eyes of Soviet agents are on some of you. I am a living lie. I am a traitor, I am a native American Communist spy. And may God have mercy on my soul.

Cheap mass fiction exhibited the same animus against communists. Mickey Spillane wrote a series of crime novels, whose hero was private investigator, Mike Hammer. *Out of the Lonely Night* (1951) sold three million copies. The villain is a communist named Oscar Deamer who, with fellow party members, attempts to murder Hammer's fiancée. The hero eventually triumphs by killing Deamer and all his associates. Hammer revels in his actions:

> I killed more people tonight than I have fingers on my hands. I shot them in cold blood and enjoyed every minute of it ... They were commies ... They were red sons-of-bitches who should have died long ago.

e) Fear of the Bomb

During the Cold War a generation of Americans lived with the fear of the bomb. The Soviet Union's explosion of an atomic weapon in 1949, its development of a thermonuclear hydrogen bomb in 1953, the advent of the long-range bomber and then ballistic missiles with nuclear warheads, ended the invulnerability of the United States to attack. Americans worried more about the effects of a nuclear blast than about the initial explosion itself. Ignorance about the impact of nuclear weapons quickly gave way to public concern as a series of tests were conducted in the Pacific and at home. In 1950 the government had chosen Nevada as a test site and in the next 13 years about 100 explosions were performed there.

  Some scientists began to recognise the harmful consequences of these tests. In particular they were concerned about the radioactive dust left in the atmosphere by a detonated weapon - so-called nuclear fallout. Radioactive particles could be carried on the wind over large distances affecting far more people than those simply present at the test site. Exposure to fallout caused radiation sickness and leukaemia, among other conditions. The unease of ordinary Americans and sections of the scientific community about fallout created a campaign to end nuclear testing. In 1957 a pressure group called SANE (National Committee for a Sane Nuclear Policy) was formed to persuade the government to terminate testing. However, in the 1950s official government scientists denied that testing posed a threat to public health and firmly opposed a ban.

Public anxiety about fallout was mirrored in contemporary culture. Tom Lehrer's satirical songs brought a dark humour to the subject.

1 And we will all go together when we go,
   Ev'ry Hottentot and ev'ry Eskimo.
   When the air becomes uranious,
   We will all go simultaneous,
5 Yes, we will all go together
   When we all go together,
   Yes, we all will go together when we go.

The science-fiction film *Them!* (1954) dealt with the genetic mutations caused by radiation. It featured mutant ants the size of buses crawling out of a New Mexico test site. In the film a scientist attributes their existence to residual radiation from the first atomic bomb. The popular film *On the Beach* (1959) was bleaker. An Australian couple and an American naval captain await the arrival of a radioactive cloud which has already destroyed all life in the northern hemisphere. The last scene of the film depicts an empty town square. The film's message was simple: there would be no survivors in a nuclear war.

The American public's horror of the atomic age was combined with fascination. Advertisers quickly capitalised on the interest in all things nuclear. The bikini was named after Bikini Atoll, the Pacific test site for America's bombs, and was so called because it was shaped like the mushroom cloud created by an atomic explosion. Sweets were named Atomic Fire Balls and the American housewife was told that the same precision-tooled machinery that drove America's nuclear submarines improved the efficiency of her kitchen refrigerator. Several comic-book characters were products of the atomic age. An atomic blast transformed scientist Bruce Banner into the Incredible Hulk, while Atom Ant was an atomic-powered superhero insect.

The possibility of a Soviet nuclear attack prompted the government to consider measures of civil defence. Numerous propaganda campaigns were launched. One urged men to wear broad-brimmed hats to counter the heat flash unleashed by a bomb. Schoolchildren were targeted too. They were urged to 'Duck and Cover' under their school desks. The 'Duck and Cover' campaign was supported by three million comic books and an animated film. The film contained a catchy jingle.

1 There was a turtle by the name of Bert.
   And Bert the Turtle was very alert.
   When danger threatened him he never got hurt.
   He knew just what to do.

5   He'd Duck and Cover. Duck and Cover.
    He did what we all must learn to do.
    You and you and you and you.
    Duck and Cover!

Pupils were subjected to regular air-raid drills. The siren would sound at noon and children would take shelter under their desks or be escorted to fallout shelters marked with black-and-yellow signs. The Federal Civil Defence Administration was founded and plans were drawn up to evacuate people from densely populated cities. Eisenhower's 1956 Interstate Act authorised the construction of an interstate motorway network designed to make the process of evacuation easier. Car-owners were advised to keep their tanks three-quarters full and ready for emergency evacuation. Individuals were also encouraged to build fallout shelters. Women's magazines suggested ideas for decorating shelters and encouraged housewives to think of them as playrooms or family dens. The government issued a standard design for a Family Fallout Shelter, but federal grants for the construction of shelters were meagre or non-existent. The building of shelters was the responsibility of the private citizen. The government paid lip-service to the idea of civil defence but in practice spent only $60 million on it between 1955 and 1960. Nevertheless, in spite of very limited subsidy, a million shelters had been built by 1960. Many were stocked with first-aid kits, tinned fruit and canned water. Families practised timed evacuations from home to shelter.

By the mid-1960s public anxiety about the bomb had subsided and much less attention was paid to civil defence. In truth there had never been a coherent national policy of civil defence and successive administrations were not prepared to finance one. A five-year programme of shelter construction proposed by Kennedy in 1961 was costed at $3.5 billion and was never implemented. There was also a growing awareness that civil defence was futile. In 1964 President Johnson spoke for many when he said, 'Victory is no longer a truth. It is only a word to describe who is left alive in the ruins.' People had become accustomed to the existence of nuclear weapons and so less frightened of them. Moreover, public concerns about fallout had been allayed by the end of atmospheric testing enshrined in the Nuclear Test Ban Treaty (1963). Fallout was no longer a focus for popular fears of the bomb.

3 Economy

a) Regional Development

Perhaps one of the most important changes in post-war American society has been the shift in wealth and population away from the north-east and mid-west to the south and west of the United States, areas known as the 'sunbelt'. Since the 1940s per capita incomes in the south and west have risen from below 75 per cent of the national average to close to the average, while those in the mid-Atlantic and Great Lakes states have dropped from well above average to close to the national norm. This process has been accelerated by the Cold War. Historically the mid-west and north-eastern states had been the crucible of America's industrial economy. Steel-producing cities like Pittsburgh in Pennsylvania and centres of car production like Detroit in Michigan formed America's industrial heartland. Yet these regions entered a period of relative economic decline and new industrial areas rose on the southern and western perimeters.

The most rapidly growing regions in the south and west were often those with a concentration of hi-tech and defence industries. They were the major beneficiaries of the growth of America's armed forces in the Cold War era and their expansion has been described as the 'rise of the gunbelt'. As the Pentagon increased its military spending, so it placed defence contracts worth millions of dollars with firms in the south and west. California with its cluster of computer, electronics and communications equipment industries quickly felt the effect. Los Angeles was chosen as the site for the production of the H-bomb in the 1950s and by the end of the decade a higher proportion of defence orders (21 per cent) were being awarded to firms in California than in any other single state. The changing technology of warfare had given new importance to the air force. The long-range bomber and ballistic missiles, both capable of delivering nuclear weapons, were vital components in a superpower's armoury, and the growth of the aerospace industry in the west mirrored the rise of the air force. California was home to the Hughes Aircraft Plant and the McDonnell-Douglas Corporation, while Bell Helicopters and the NASA space centre were based in Houston, Texas. The prosperity of the city of Seattle in the Pacific north-west partly rested on the fact that it was the headquarters of aircraft manufacturer Boeing.

High military spending by federal government was by no means the only reason for the economic growth of the periphery. The decline of traditional industries elsewhere prompted workers to move to the south and west in search of employment. Moreover, by no means all government spending was funnelled to southern and western states. Defence industries also flourished in older states like New Hampshire, Connecticut and Massachusetts. Besides, the spectacular growth of southern cities like Atlanta, Georgia had very little to do with defence production. However, higher levels of defence spending during the Cold War were undoubtedly a contributory factor in America's changing patterns of wealth, population distribution and industrial geography.

b) Cost of the Cold War, 1945-63

The cost of the Cold War was a persistent source of concern to politicians. Prior to the Second World War the United States had an army smaller than Romania's, no intelligence service and a small arms manufacturing base. Yet the Cold War forced the United States to allocate substantial financial and human resources to national defence. The foundations of a much larger military establishment were laid in 1947, although significant increases in the defence budget did not actually occur until American intervention in Korea. The National Security Act created the National Security Council and the CIA and merged the War and Navy Departments into a single Defence Department housed in the Pentagon Building in Washington. Participation in the Korean War underlined that America's post-war definition of national security was far more ambitious and wide-ranging than in the past: national security meant more than defending America's natural frontiers, it required the deployment of American forces to defend the 'free world' against the menace of communism. At the end of the Korean War in 1953 the United States had 3.2 million men under arms, the largest intelligence agency in the world, and was spending 14.4 per cent of its gross national product (GNP) on defence. President Eisenhower in particular worried about the burden imposed by defence spending and chose it as the theme for his farewell address to the American people in 1961.

1 Our military organisation today bears little resemblance to that
   known by any of my predecessors in peacetime ... Until the latest
   of our world conflicts, the United States had no armaments
   industry ... But now ... we have been compelled to create a
5 permanent armaments industry of vast proportions. Added to this,
   three and a half million men and women are directly engaged in the
   defence establishment. We annually spend more on military
   security than the net income of all United States corporations.
      This conjunction of an immense military establishment and a
10 large arms industry is new in the American experience. The total
   influence ... is felt in every city, every state house, every office of
   the federal government ...
      In the councils of government we must guard against the
   acquisition of unwarranted influence, whether sought or unsought,
15 by the military industrial complex. The potential for the disastrous
   rise of misplaced power exists and will persist.
      We must never let the weight of this combination endanger our
   liberties or democratic processes. We should take nothing for
   granted. Only an alert and knowledgeable citizenry can compel the
20 proper meshing of the huge military and industrial machinery of
   defence with our peaceful methods and goals, so that security and
   liberty may prosper together.

Two fears were implicit in the speech. One was a fear of the military-industrial complex. Eisenhower warned that the armed forces and America's defence industries were dangerously interdependent. Both had a vested interest in ever higher levels of military spending and served as powerful pressure groups in Washington lobbying for increases in the defence budget. Leaders of the armed services would always want more men and equipment, while industrialists would always want more defence contracts and correspondingly higher profits. Military chiefs and industrialists had a shared interest in exaggerating the threat to national security in order to squeeze more funds from the government. Often the sort of increases demanded were simply not warranted by the actual threat. Eisenhower believed that what was in the interests of the military and defence manufacturers was not necessarily in the interests of the civilian population.

Eisenhower's other related fear was that waging the Cold War would turn America into a warfare or garrison state. The main characteristics of a garrison state were a condition of perpetual military alert, compulsory military service, consistently high levels of defence spending supported by a regime of high taxation, and state controls on industry to ensure output targets in certain industrial sectors were met. All this compromised the fundamental American principles of individual liberty and minimal state intervention in the market.

Is there good evidence for the sort of military-industrial complex identified by Eisenhower? The real level of defence spending and the proportion of GNP consumed by the military are two reasonable indicators. Defence spending reached a peak in 1953 during the Korean War. Thereafter it decreased continuously with the exception of modest rises in 1957 and under Kennedy in 1961 and 1962, but even the higher levels of spending in those years were significantly below the figure for 1953. The 1953 level of spending was only once repeated at the height of the Vietnam War in 1968. The defence budget also accounted for a diminishing share of GNP after the end of the Korean War. In 1953 it took up nearly 14 per cent of GNP but subsequently its share of GNP never exceeded 10 per cent and was sometimes lower. If the military-industrial complex had operated as Eisenhower suggested, then we might have expected spending on the military to have accounted for a constantly growing proportion of GNP. It must, however, be remembered that not only lower real defence spending but also healthy economic growth explain the smaller share of GNP consumed by military expenditure. For most of the period covered by this book, with the exception of the years 1958-60, the United States enjoyed high economic growth.

There is also limited evidence that the United States developed into a garrison state under the influence of the Cold War. There was gradual demobilisation after the Korean War. The size of the US armed forces peaked in 1953 at 3.2 million. Under Eisenhower there was a steady fall in the number of active peacetime military personnel to 2.4 million, followed by a slight increase under Kennedy to 2.7 million. Nor was a system of universal conscription ever introduced. In spite of the support of presidents, plans to introduce universal military training (UMT) were defeated in Congress. The basic reason was a deep-rooted American hostility to compulsion. UMT would have required every young American male to undergo a period of military training and would have created a vast pool of reserve manpower. Instead America's manpower needs were met by the draft or selective service. Under this system every male had to register his availability for military service but those who served were chosen by lot. There was an element of compulsion in selective service and it was a break with the tradition of a small volunteer army, but the lottery system seemed more acceptable to a society with no history of conscription until the Second World War (apart from a brief period during the American Civil War). Finally the Cold War did not mean high levels of personal taxation for Americans. There were no general increases in tax rates during the 1950s other than those voted to cover the emergency costs of the Korean War. Even higher defence spending under Kennedy was not accompanied by increases in personal taxation. Indeed Kennedy planned cuts in personal income tax which were eventually introduced after his death in 1964.

Both Truman and Eisenhower must take some credit for placing a cap on military spending. Resistance to larger defence budgets came from the very top. In spite of worsening relations with the Soviet Union, Truman opposed allocating more funds to the armed services until the Korean War made it necessary. Privately he worried about the militarisation of American society. Although Korea brought about permanently higher levels of defence expenditure, Eisenhower too consistently refused the armed services' demands for further expansion in the 1950s. When General Maxwell Taylor proposed the enlargement of the army to 28 divisions in 1956, Eisenhower 'had nearly fainted'. The attitude of both Truman and Eisenhower was partly dictated by political considerations. Higher defence spending presupposed higher taxes. It also ran the risk of inflation which would necessitate the introduction of wage and price controls. Although they had been accepted by Americans during the Second World War as a necessary short-term sacrifice in order to defeat Fascism, they had been deeply unpopular. They would be even less popular in peacetime. But Truman and Eisenhower also opposed bigger defence budgets on ideological grounds. Universal conscription, higher taxes and federal controls threatened the established American principles of personal freedom, low personal taxation and a free market. Eisenhower in particular was not prepared to wage the Cold War at the expense of historic American liberties. He warned the National Security Council in 1953 that if America's armed forces were continuously expanded, 'it would be necessary to resort to compulsory controls and ... out-and-out regimentation. We could lick the whole world ... if we were willing to adopt the system of Adolf Hitler.'

The cost of the Cold War was massive. In 1955, for example, $42.4 billion out of a total federal budget of $68.4 billion was spent on the armed forces. Even a nation as wealthy as the United States found the economic demands of superpower status increasingly burdensome. In spite of Eisenhower's attempts to balance the budget, defence spending contributed to sizeable budget deficits between 1958 and 1960. Those deficits continued under Kennedy and his successors. The average size of the budget deficit in the 1960s was $6 billion. Unlike Eisenhower, Kennedy was prepared to run a deficit, but the point is that America could no longer pay for the Cold War without incurring budget deficits. Nevertheless, throughout the period 1945-63 the United States fought the Cold War without bankrupting itself, without imposing high personal taxes and without having to sacrifice the production of ordinary consumer goods. America did not become a garrison state and was able to afford both guns and butter. The relevant comparison is with the Soviet Union. Between 1947 and 1963 defence spending averaged 9 per cent of US GNP. By contrast the Soviet Union consumed 25 per cent of its GNP, which was in any case only about one-third of the size of America's, on military expenditure. Consequently the Soviet Union has been described as only an 'incomplete superpower'. America's higher rates of economic growth enabled it to sustain the Cold War, whereas ultimately relative Soviet economic weakness was a major reason for the collapse of the Soviet Union and the end of the Cold War.

Making notes on '*Home Front: the Impact of the Cold War on the United States, 1945-63*'

This is a long and diverse chapter and you should pay attention to the headings within the chapter and the summary diagram at the end as an aid to note-taking. It would be a good idea to divide your notes into three separate sections, Politics, Society and Economy. In the first section you should trace the growing powers of the presidency in the Cold War era. Concentrate on the extension of the president's war- and treaty-making powers. Then try to link the enlargement of those powers to the progress of the Cold War. Under 'Society' you may want to describe briefly the 'Red Scare' and the activities of Senator McCarthy. Make sure you can define the term 'McCarthyism'. You should then examine the principal causes and consequences of McCarthyism. Next you might consider a different issue and examine for what reasons and with what consequences there was a pervasive fear of nuclear war within the United States in the 1960s. When taking notes under the heading 'Economy', you might find the following questions helpful. What was the effect of the Cold War defence boom on regional economic development? What is meant by the terms 'military-industrial complex' and 'garrison state'? What evidence is there for and against the development of both? To what extent was the Cold War affordable for the United States in this period?

Summary - Home Front: The Impact of the Cold War on the United States, 1945-63

Answering essays on 'Home Front: The Impact of the Cold War on the United States, 1945-63'

The following questions on the domestic effects of the Cold War illustrate the likely main issues for examiners.

1   How and why did presidential powers grow as a result of the Cold War between 1947 and 1963?
2   Account for the impact of Senator Joseph McCarthy on US political life.
3   Examine the effects of McCarthyism on American society in the 1950s.
4   For what reasons and with what results was there a widespread fear of nuclear war among Americans in the 1950s?
5   Analyse the effects of the Cold War on the US economy between 1947 and 1963.

You have encountered all these question types in previous chapters. You ought therefore to have some idea about how to approach these questions. As for content, let us look at questions 1 and 5. For the first part of question 1 examine the changing balance of power between Congress and the presidency and try to identify landmarks in the growth of the power of the executive. You might also wish to introduce and define the term 'imperial presidency'. In the second section of your answer you should try to trace the increasing powers of the president to developments in the Cold War. Question 5 gives you plenty of scope. You are examining a broad area across a long time-span. In order to give your essay structure and direction, you must analyse the impact of the Cold War on particular areas of the US economy. What effect did the Cold War have on regional development, defence spending in absolute terms and as a percentage of GNP, on the federal budget and on levels of taxation? You might also consider the evidence for and against a military-industrial complex.

Source-based questions on 'Home Front: The Impact of the Cold War on the United States, 1945-63'

Eisenhower's Farewell Address
Read the extract on page 142 and answer the following questions.
a)   In the context of the extract explain the meaning of the following terms. i) 'the defence establishment' (line 7); (1 mark) ii) 'the military industrial complex' (line 15). (1 mark)
b)   Using both the extract and your own knowledge, comment on the validity of Eisenhower's claim that a military-industrial complex existed in the United States by 1961. (8 marks)

Chronological Table

1945

February	Yalta Conference
April	Death of FDR. Truman became president
August	US dropped A-bombs on Hiroshima and Nagasaki
	Potsdam Conference
	Japanese surrender and US military occupation of Japan

1946

February	Kennan's Long Telegram
March	Churchill's 'Iron Curtain' speech
September	Wallace dismissed from Truman cabinet
November	Congress passed Atomic Energy Act

1947

March	Truman Doctrine announced
June	Marshall Plan announced
September	National Security Act

1948

June	Berlin Airlift began
August	South Korea established
November	Truman re-elected as president

1949

April	NATO established
May	Berlin blockade ended by Soviet Union
September	Federal Republic of Germany established
	Soviet Union successfully tested A-bomb
October	Chinese communists won civil war. People's Republic of China established

German Democratic Republic established

1950

February	Senator McCarthy alleged that 205 communists were working within State Department
March	NSC 68
	US initiated aid to French in the war against the Vietminh
June	North Korea invaded South Korea
	US sent troops to South Korea
	Resumption of aid to Jiang on Taiwan
September	MacArthur landed at Inchon
	Internal Security Act
November	China entered Korean War

1951

April	Truman dismissed MacArthur
September	US signed peace treaty and mutual security pact with Japan

1952

November	Republican Eisenhower elected president

1953

March	Death of Stalin
July	Mossadeq overthrown as prime minister in Iran after CIA intervention
	Korean armistice

1954

May	French defeated by Vietminh at Dien Bien Phu
June	CIA-backed coup ousted Arbenz from power in Guatemala
July	Geneva Acccords on Vietnam

	US opened military mission in South Vietnam
September	Beginning of first Chinese offshore islands crisis
December	McCarthy censured in the Senate

1955

| May | West Germany admitted to NATO |
| July | Geneva summit |

1956

November	Hungarian uprising
	Suez crisis
	Eisenhower re-elected as president

1957

| October | Soviet Union launched Sputnik |

1958

July	US Marines landed in Lebanon
August	Second Chinese offshore islands crisis
November	Khrushchev issued ultimatum over Berlin

1959

| January | Castro seized power in Cuba |
| September | Khrushchev visited United States |

1960

May	Gary Powers shot down in U-2 over Soviet Union
June	Abortive Paris summit
November	Democrat Kennedy elected president
December	National Liberation Front formed in South Vietnam

1961

| January | US severed relations with Cuba |

Further Reading

If having read a particular chapter, you want to know more, you should refer first to the books mentioned in the first section of the bibliography. The books cited in other sections are also useful but are specialist works to be consulted at a more advanced stage in your study of the Cold War.

1 Surveys of the Cold War, 1945-63

There is a vast range of literature on the Cold War. The following books are all good starting-points for the student interested in wider reading and offer broad coverage of US policy in this period. **Martin Walker**, *The Cold War and the Making of the Modern World* (Vintage, 1994), is a thoughtful and very readable book, which really makes the Cold War come alive. Well worth reading. **Walter LaFeber**, *The American Age* (Norton, 2nd edition 1994), is also an excellent introduction to US foreign policy. Alternatively, you might try **Stephen E. Ambrose**, *Rise to Globalism: American Foreign Policy since 1938* (Penguin, 1988). Another student-friendly text is **Ralph B. Levering**, *The Cold War: A Post-Cold War History* (Harlan Davidson, 1994). **Akira Iriye and Warren I. Cohen (eds)** *Cambridge History of Foreign Relations* Vol. IV (Cambridge, 1993), also provides a clear overview of US foreign policy during the Cold War. **James T. Patterson**, *Grand Expectations: The United States 1945-74* (Oxford, 1996), is essentially a domestic history of the United States, but it also contains concise and lively chapters on the beginnings of the Cold War and on how successive presidents managed the conflict. It is a superb book which is both accessible and scholarly. **Christopher Andrew**, *For the President's Eyes Only* (Harper Collins, 1995), is an authoritative work on the intelligence history of the Cold War. **John Ranelagh**, *The Agency: The Rise and Decline of the CIA,* (BBC, 1987), is a general introduction to the activities of the CIA. **John Dumbrell**, *The Making of US Foreign Policy* (Manchester, 1990), offers a clear analysis of the foreign policy making process in the United States discussed in Chapter 1. Students wanting to know more about the domestic political context should consult the invaluable **R.V. Dennenberg**, *Understanding American Politics* (Fontana, 1984).

The following books cover a broad range but are less accessible. A very rewarding book is **Richard Crockatt**, *The Fifty Years War* (Routledge, 1995), which examines the Cold War from both the US and Soviet perspectives. The more ambitious student might also try **John Gaddis**, *The Long Peace: Inquiries into the History of the Cold War* (Oxford, 1987), which is a thought-provoking collection of essays on different aspects of the Cold War. The same author's *Strategies of Containment* (Oxford, 1982) is also a masterly study of the origins and evolution of the containment doctrine and contains many useful extracts from primary sources.

2 Origins of the Cold War

There is a wealth of historiography on this topic. **Thomas G. Patterson and Robert J. McMahon (eds.),** *The Origins of the Cold War* (Heath, 1991), contains essays by different authors on many different facets of the beginning of the Cold War. **Melvyn P. Leffler and David S. Painter (eds),** T*he Origins of the Cold War: An International History* (Routledge, 1994), and **David Reynolds (ed.),** *The Origins of the Cold War in Europe* (Yale, 1994), are similar books. Probably the most important book to be published recently on the origins and early history of the Cold War is **Melvyn P. Leffler,** *A Preponderance of Power: National Security, the Truman Administration and the Cold War* (Stanford, 1992). Leffler has exploited newly declassified sources and has virtually rewritten the history of the beginning of the Cold War at least from the American side. The contents of this vast and dense book are presented in more palatable form in the same author's brief *The Spectre of Communism, The United States and the Origins of the Cold War* (Hill and Wang, 1994), which is designed as an aid for students.

3 The Cold War 1947-53

Both of Leffler's books cover events in both Europe and Asia in this period very well. **Michael Schaller,** *The United States and China in the Twentieth Century* (Oxford, 1990), is very good on US policy during the Chinese civil war and its aftermath. **John W. Dower,** *Japan in War and Peace* (New Press, 1993), has excellent essays on the importance of Japan in the early Cold War.

4 Eisenhower and the Cold War

Stephen E. Ambrose, *Eisenhower The President* (Allen and Unwin, 1983), examines Ike's leadership during the Cold War in depth. **Eisenhower's** own two volumes of memoirs, *Mandate for Change,* (Heinemann, 1963), and *Waging Peace* (Heinemann, 1965), are also a useful source for the historian. **Robert A. Divine,** *Eisenhower and the Cold War* (Oxford, 1981), has much useful material on the 'New Look', US policy in Asia, wide-ranging coverage of American actions in the Middle East and a valuable chapter on Eisenhower's diplomacy with the Soviet Union. **Michael R. Beschloss,** *Mayday: Eisenhower, Khrushchev and the U-2 Affair* (Faber, 1986), is more than just a fascinating study of the U-2 programme and Powers's last flight. It also sets US-Soviet relations between 1956 and 1960 in a broad historical context.

5 Kennedy and the Cold War

Kennedy remains an alluring figure and his life has generated numerous biographies. **Michael R. Beschloss**, *Kennedy versus Khrushchev: The Crisis Years 1961-63* (Faber, 1991), has a wealth of personal detail about Kennedy and his approach to foreign policy, but is also a detailed study of US-Soviet relations under Kennedy. The Cuban missile crisis has also attracted an extensive literature. One of the best recent studies is **Mark J. White**, *The Cuban Missile Crisis* (Macmillan, 1996). **Robert Smith Thompson**, *The Missiles of October* (South Carolina, 1992), skilfully uses recently declassified sources to tell an exciting story well. **Robert Kennedy's** posthumous *Thirteen Days* (Norton, 1969), offers the view of one of the participants. **Stanley Karnow**, *Vietnam: A History* (Viking, 1983), analyses well the shortcomings of US policy in Vietnam under Kennedy.

6 The Cold War at Home

Arthur M. Schlesinger Jr. presents his theory of an imperial presidency in his *The Imperial Presidency* (Houghton Mifflin, 1973). **John Dumbrell**, *The Making of US Foreign Policy* (Manchester, 1990), explains the changing balance of power between the presidency and Congress. The cultural impact of the Cold War is covered well by **Stephen J. Whitfield** in *The Culture of the Cold War* (Baltimore, 1991), which has an interesting section on the imprint left by the Cold War on popular fiction and the cinema. There are some fine studies of the McCarthy era, including **Richard M. Fried**, *Nightmare in Red* (Oxford 1990). The fear of nuclear war and fallout is covered by **Alan Winkler**, *Life under a Cloud: American Anxiety about the Atom* (Oxford, 1993). **Anne Markusen et al.**, *The Rise of the Gunbelt* (Oxford, 1991), analyses the effects of the defence boom on the US economy and considers the issue of the military-industrial complex.

Index